"This book is a good, quick recounting of the life and ministry of Dr. Martyn Lloyd-Jones from one who knew him personally. Christopher Catherwood, the Doctor's eldest grandchild, puts the books you've enjoyed in the context of Lloyd-Jones's life and ministry. The author carefully and fairly interprets Lloyd-Jones—even on points where he himself may disagree. He succeeds in faithfully reproducing some of the Doctor's nuances and ambiguities that others have overlooked. The book's informal, even casual style makes it easy to read—like you're having an engaging evening's conversation with an old friend. I heartily commend the books and sermons of Martyn-Lloyd Jones, and this book as an encouragement and help."

Mark Dever, Senior Pastor, Capitol Hill Baptist Church, Washington, DC; President, 9Marks

"God is raising up a new generation of preachers who aim faithfully to expound the Scriptures in the Reformed heritage, who are passionate about evangelism, who talk up justification and sanctification, who are eager to plant churches in challenging contexts. They want and need models—ideally, not because they want to become thoughtless clones, but because the Bible itself helps us see how much is learned by imitation. One of the crucially important models of the twentieth century is Martyn Lloyd-Jones, whose homegoing in 1981 is just far enough back that a new generation of young preachers does not automatically know him. May this brief, balanced, and personal biography of Lloyd-Jones, written by one of his grandsons, go a long way to providing the incentive to study him afresh, to listen or read his sermons, and thus to increase the circle of those we should emulate in gospel faithfulness."

D. A. Carson, Research Professor of New Testament, Trinity Evangelical Divinity School

"For many people who heard him, Dr. Martyn Lloyd-Jones was perhaps the greatest preacher in the English language in the twentieth century. He possessed a rare gift of communicating the truth, wonder, and power of the gospel. His grandson Christopher Catherwood had the privilege of seeing the inner man. In this absorbing book he brings a fresh perspective on the Doctor's life and the convictions that shaped his long and fruitful ministry. Those who heard him preach will be reminded of the ministry of this prince of preachers. One also hopes that many who never heard him will be encouraged to read his books and listen to his sermons. Those who do so will not be disappointed."

Lindsay Brown, International Director, the Lausanne Movement

"We hear a great deal today about the need to be relevant. What the Doctor so powerfully demonstrated through his preaching and books is that to be always relevant one must be *biblical*. My hope is that this first-rate book will introduce a new generation of readers to Dr. Martyn Lloyd-Jones, whose message and methodology is as relevant and needed today as it was in his time."

Rebecca Manley Pippert, speaker; evangelist; author, *Out of the Salt*

"This excellent introduction to Martyn Lloyd-Jones's life and ministry will not only introduce many to one of the preaching giants of the last century but also inspire us to apply the convictions he held so passionately to our present day. We may well disagree with him at points, as his own grandson admits to doing, but his radical commitment to the principle of *sola scriptura*, in both doctrine and practice, is urgently needed today."

Vaughan Roberts, Rector of St Ebbe's Oxford and Director of The Proclamation Trust

MARTYN LLOYD-JONES

MARTYN LLOYD-JONES

HIS LIFE AND RELEVANCE FOR THE 21ST CENTURY

CHRISTOPHER CATHERWOOD

WHEATON, ILLINOIS

Martyn Lloyd-Jones: His Life and Relevance for the 21st Century

Copyright © 2015 by Christopher Catherwood

Published by Crossway
        1300 Crescent Street
        Wheaton, Illinois 60187

Cover design: Josh Dennis

Cover image: Lady Elizabeth Catherwood and Christopher Catherwood

First printing 2015

Printed in the United States of America

Trade paperback ISBN: 978-1-4335-4595-5
ePub ISBN: 978-1-4335-4598-6
PDF ISBN: 978-1-4335-4596-2
Mobipocket ISBN: 978-1-4335-4597-9

Library of Congress Cataloging-in-Publication Data
Catherwood, Christopher.
   Martyn Lloyd-Jones : his life and relevance for the
21st century / Christopher Catherwood.
      pages cm.
   Includes bibliographical references and index.
   ISBN 978-1-4335-4595-5 (tp)
   1. Lloyd-Jones, David Martyn. 2. Reformed
Church—Doctrines. I. Title.
BX4827.L68C38   2015
285.8092—dc23 [B]   2015001445

Crossway is a publishing ministry of Good News Publishers.

VP		25	24	23	22	21	20	19	18	17	16	15
15	14	13	12	11	10	9	8	7	6	5	4	3	2	1

To Don and Emilie,
a Reformed pastor and his wife
in the mold of Martyn and Bethan Lloyd-Jones,
and to their friend,
my wife Paulette,
to whom Bethan Lloyd-Jones commented,
"Martyn would have liked you."

Contents

1

Martyn Lloyd-Jones

A MAN FOR ALL TIMES

"I thought he was a friend of Spurgeon's!"

I will never forget that incredible statement by a fellow student in the Oxford Inter-Collegiate Christian Union who was astonished to find that Dr. Martyn Lloyd-Jones was not only still alive but preaching for the OICCU later that term. He was, at that time, very much alive.

That is now more than forty years ago. He lived until 1981, and his books have sold in enormous numbers since his death, as they did during his lifetime. But while many of today's Christians have heard of him, not everyone knows that much about him. Nor have they necessarily read any of his books.

Yet today, there is a huge new interest in Reformed theology, of the same kind that Dr. Lloyd-Jones himself encouraged after the Second World War. Movements like Together for the Gospel and The Gospel Coalition, as well as the growing enthusiasm through evangelical leaders such as John Piper, Mark Dever, Tim Keller, and others for thoughtful, Scripture-centered, rigorous Christianity, all show that something remarkable is happening.

Listen to what Iain Murray has to say, in quoting an Australian

Christian leader who knew Martyn Lloyd-Jones and heard him preach:

> In an extraordinary way, the presence of God was in that church. I personally felt as if a hand were pushing me through the pew. At the end of the sermon for some reason or other the organ did not play, the Doctor went off into the vestry [his office around the back] and everyone sat completely still without moving. It must have been almost ten minutes before people seemed to find the strength to get up and, without speaking to one another, quietly leave the church. Never have I witnessed or experienced such preaching with such fantastic reaction on the part of the congregation.[1]

As John Piper says about Lloyd-Jones's preaching in general:

> The sermon is a word from God, through a man. I am deeply thankful to God that he led me to Lloyd-Jones in 1968. He has been a constant reminder: you don't have to be cool, hip, or clever to be powerful. In fact, the sacred anointing is simply in another world from those communication techniques. His is the world I want to live in when I step into the pulpit.[2]

Is that a world you would want to live in? If so, this book is for you as it describes not just the life but also the thought of a man whose regular preaching profoundly affected his hearers. As John Piper and others attest, becoming familiar with Dr. Lloyd-Jones could transform your life.

While not everyone is as excited as some of us at the renewed enthusiasm for Reformed theology, even those who are cautious revere and look up to the achievements of Martyn Lloyd-Jones. As we shall see, not everyone agrees with "the Doctor," as he was called, on everything. But all agree that he is as relevant in the early

---

[1] Iain H. Murray, *David Martyn Lloyd-Jones: The Fight of Faith, 1939–1981* (Edinburgh: Banner of Truth, 1990), 377.

[2] John Piper, "A Passion for Christ-Exalting Power: Martyn Lloyd-Jones on the Need for Revival and Baptism with the Holy Spirit" (paper presented at the Bethlehem Fourth Annual Conference for Pastors, January 30, 1991). See also D. Martyn Lloyd-Jones, *Preaching and Preachers*, ed. Kevin DeYoung (Grand Rapids, MI: Zondervan, 2011), 153–55.

twenty-first century as he was when he was alive during most of the twentieth.

One of the hallmarks of this new movement is a renewed interest in the giants of the past. Students are reading John Owen and Jonathan Edwards in ways that would have been unthinkable until recently. No one was more enthusiastic for the works of such illustrious evangelical forebears than Martyn Lloyd-Jones himself. So it is appropriate that people are now rediscovering his works as well.

As we shall see, he always considered himself more an enthusiast for the eighteenth century than the seventeenth, and that is significant. Martyn Lloyd-Jones was a brilliant man, but his preaching was not merely cerebral. He called preaching "logic on fire."[3] He despised histrionics, and his sermons were always reasoned and thought through. But they reflected the warmth and inner passions of the man within and were felt with genuine emotion or true fire. The Welsh, his people, have never been scared of true emotion, and neither was he.

This is evident in his preaching style: he spoke with passionate appeal to believers and nonbelievers alike. He was not afraid to raise his voice dramatically when proclaiming the truth. His was not the calm, quiet, dispassionate voice of many an Anglican preacher of the day. But compared with other Welsh Free Church preachers of his time he was mild in his delivery. Download one of his sermons and hear him today![4]

Indeed, since interest in the life and works of Martyn Lloyd-Jones does seem to be part of the great Reformed renaissance in North America and elsewhere, there is surely a place for a book like this. That is not to say that *he* would of necessity have been a supporter of the current exciting trends—one of the themes of this book is that one cannot say what a man who died in 1981 would or would not have thought of events over three decades after his death. But for those who are now discovering the wonderful truths of the theology that fired great men such as George Whitefield,

---

[3] Lloyd-Jones, *Preaching and Preachers*, 110.
[4] To listen to or to download a sermon visit MLJ Trust at http://www.mljtrust.org/sermons/.

John Owen, Jonathan Edwards, Charles Spurgeon, and countless Puritans and their eighteenth- and nineteenth-century successors, a study of Martyn Lloyd-Jones is surely necessary.

This therefore is *not* a conventional biography. Others have written such books for different audiences. Serious and objective academic studies on the subject of the Doctor are available, such as *Engaging with Martyn Lloyd-Jones*. *The Christ-Centred Preaching of Martyn Lloyd-Jones* is a selection of sermons that I and the Doctor's elder daughter Elizabeth chose to give a flavor of the kind of preaching that made him so internationally loved and well known.[5]

My relationship to the Doctor (as his eldest grandchild) is not directly relevant to this book. My goal is to introduce him to a new generation of readers and to help those discovering wonderful biblical truths for the first time learn how to think *scripturally* for themselves as Christians. This book is as much about the kind of evangelical mind that Lloyd-Jones possessed, and the way in which he went about his daily life before God, as what he did and when. He felt that if one was biblical, one was always relevant, and that is as true in the twenty-first century as it was in the twentieth or eighteenth.

He was, of course, a man of his own time, ordained by God to live from 1899 to 1981 and to reach out to people in that time span. But while it might be true to say, as some have in recent days, that no one in the Internet age would listen to a ninety-minute sermon, the *principles* of what Dr. Lloyd-Jones preached are surely as relevant as ever. It is not the length of his preaching that matters but what underlies it.

When he stepped into the pulpit every Sunday morning and evening and every Friday night in Westminster Chapel, there was a hush and sense of expectation. His black Geneva gown hid him as an individual and drew attention to why he was there: to give his

---

[5] Andrew Atherstone and David Ceri Jones, eds., *Engaging with Martyn Lloyd-Jones: The Life and Legacy of "The Doctor"* (Nottingham: Apollos, 2011); Martyn Lloyd-Jones, *The Christ-Centered Preaching of Martyn Lloyd-Jones: Classic Sermons for the Church Today*, ed. Elizabeth Catherwood and Christopher Catherwood (Wheaton, IL: Crossway, 2014).

hearers a real sense of the presence of God through the preaching of God's Word, the Bible.

In the pulpit, he was serious. Outside it, he was often warm and funny, but so important was his message when he preached that he had a serious demeanor that everyone noticed. That was counterintuitive even in his time, when famous preachers were known for their flamboyance, literary allusions, and jokes. But the eternal destiny of the human race left no time for frivolity! And he communicated that to his congregation the moment he donned his black robe and entered the pulpit.

My previous portraits have been designed to show the Doctor's human side. While outwardly reserved (and perhaps slightly shy), the kindness and enthusiasm he always possessed were very much there to see, for the wider world as well as for his family and close inner circle. He had what is often called a gift for friendship. He also had an infectious sense of humor that, while not present in his sermons, was evident in all his dealings with others. But my intent here is to present him as a preacher in whom one could sense the presence of the Holy Spirit—what the Puritans called *unction*— and to show how the Doctor's message is as relevant today as it was then.

While this is more an objective rather than a personal study, some of the insights gained through my family relationship with him are nonetheless relevant. He was someone who loved debate and discussion. When it came to spiritual issues, he always emphasized to his descendants that what we believe, if we are Christians, must be *Bible-based* and viable from Scripture. He always preferred us to hold to our beliefs *for ourselves*, not because we were his grandchildren.

Obviously on nonnegotiable doctrines like the cross and resurrection, true Christians are and must be in unanimity. In one sense, if one has a different interpretation of what Lloyd-Jones and Luther called *secondary issues*, it does not matter. Lloyd-Jones recognized as fellow evangelicals people with different views from himself on many issues, such as the one that provides the context for our book: Reformed theology. He himself zealously held to the way that John Calvin, the Puritans, and eighteenth-century heroes such as Edwards and Whitefield interpreted many key scriptural passages. But so long as those who disagreed, including giants of the faith such as John Wesley, did so on biblical grounds, that was fine with him. Arminians could be evangelicals too.

Not everyone might agree, for instance, with his views on music in church—he scrapped the choir in the churches in which he was the pastor. But while music is often a source of much argument within a church, it is, compared to issues of salvation and the authority of Scripture, a decidedly secondary issue. (We will look at this issue in chap. 5.)

In other words, I am putting him forward as a role model but not as an icon. As an evangelical Protestant, he did not believe in the pope or in papal infallibility. He was horrified when people tried to put him on a platform or pedestal, because he was very aware, as any real Christian should be, of his own fallibility and human frailty. He did of course hold his beliefs very zealously indeed. But I can say that he never saw himself as six feet above contradiction.

What, therefore, can the Doctor teach us today? What is his permanent relevance to a new group of people discovering biblical truths for themselves for the first time? Even if the renaissance in Reformed thought is short, at least one generation will benefit from being grounded in the kind of theology upon which Martyn Lloyd-Jones based his own ministry, as did Owen, Whitefield, and Spurgeon in their own times.

Such figures never go away. Some of us are fortunate to be part of the Francis Schaeffer/L'Abri age group. But while that movement is not as eminent now as it was back in the 1960s and '70s, what Francis Schaeffer wrote and taught halfway up a Swiss mountain is often rediscovered today. It is interesting that many current L'Abri staff workers never met the man himself, yet find him as relevant as he was in his own lifetime.

One prays that it will be the same for the life and works of Martyn Lloyd-Jones. The truths he expounded so faithfully from the pulpit and in his books are eternal. The principles upon which he based everything were from the Bible and so remain forever. May he inspire new generations of Christians to become as excited and enthusiastic for the great things of God as he was.

So the next two chapters will provide an overview of his life, for those who are unfamiliar with such details. With a life so full, I had to be selective. The goal of these chapters is to tie in to the main themes that we will explore in more depth later in the book, and to provide the biographical framework for an analysis of his thought, writing, and twenty-first century relevance.

With many eminent people, such as Winston Churchill, biographies often begin with the subject as the hero. Then he or she becomes the villain. And then with the passing of time more objective works are written, as the great seventeenth-century British leader Oliver Cromwell put it, "warts and all," with the heroics and faults balanced to provide an even picture.

My aim, however, is to show how profoundly relevant his life and thinking are to us as evangelicals in the twenty-first century. As the saying goes, if one is biblical, one is always relevant. Of few people is that more true than with Dr. Lloyd-Jones.

There is one difference between this work and *The Christ-Centered Preaching of Martyn Lloyd-Jones*. That book avoided the two areas of the Doctor's life that have been controversial: his views on the baptism and gifts of the Holy Spirit, and his call in 1966 for evangelicals in denominations that were theologically mixed doctrinally to separate and make their prime association with other evangelicals in fellowships of like-minded churches.

In both cases the Doctor's views have been misunderstood and perhaps even misrepresented, however sincerely, by both those who agreed with him and those who believed his stance was a major mistake.

My own position is that I agree with him on one of these areas and disagree on the other. But this book will aim to present an objective view. It does not try to convince readers that one view is right, or that Dr. Lloyd-Jones was right (or wrong) on these two issues. Rather, it demonstrates how he thought, how he came to his conclusions, and how *that* is an example to twenty-first-century evangelicals in aiding us in our own interpretation of what Scripture teaches and how central Scripture should be to all that we think, say, or do. In that sense my own views are secondary, and the reader's interpretation might be different.

Lastly, what kind of man was the Doctor? What was at the heart of his ministry? A discussion on whether he was primarily an expositor or a doctor brings out some interesting sides to his character that are worth revisiting.

At the Doctor's memorial service in 1981 an amicable dispute broke out between two of the speakers on what had influenced their late friend's preaching the most. His old friend Omri Jenkins insisted that Dr. Lloyd-Jones was an expositor first and last. Dr. Gaius Davies, a leading London psychiatrist and family friend, was surely right to say that God used the Doctor's *medical* training to make Martyn Lloyd-Jones into the kind of preacher that he later became. Medicine influenced his preaching. Sin was diagnosed as the disease, and Christ was the only remedy.

When one thinks of Lloyd-Jones's great definition of preaching— *logic on fire; theology coming through a man who is on fire*—one can clearly see that the diagnostic method he learned as a medical student at Bart's led him to the logic with which he would dissect sin and expound doctrines as so clearly laid out in Scripture. His logical and passionate preaching is what made him so unique and persuasive; one can easily see why God sent him to medical school first before he contemplated the ministry.

Doctors hope to acquire a good bedside manner of actually listening to patients in order to help come to a correct diagnosis. This is also superb training for the pastoral ministry. The Doctor was someone who *listened* and did so patiently and caringly. How often do we rush to false conclusions without hearing the other person! The Doctor did not make that mistake. People felt heard, and those who know that they have been understood are far more likely to take the wise pastoral advice given to them than those who are made to feel rushed or that they are a time-wasting nuisance.

The Doctor listened to a far wider range of people during his ministry than simply his flocks in Aberavon and London. He had a major role in the International Fellowship of Evangelical Students, being its crucial founder-chairman and then its president. People from what we now call two-thirds world countries did not always feel heard by white men, but they certainly did by the Doctor (who, as a Welshman, rather empathized with them about English colonialism).

Similarly, when he became the pastor's pastor of the wider Westminster Fellowship, his medically trained ability to listen played a crucial role in assisting the dozens of pastors who looked to him for guidance and support. This often had to be done over the telephone, but it was medical bedside-manner pastoral concern nonetheless.

Doctors often have to cut to the chase if they are to save a patient's life. Getting straight to the main point after a careful diagnosis is part of their medical training. Those of us with humanities degrees can often waffle around a subject, but not a medical doctor. This was true of Dr. Lloyd-Jones: his sermons are models of crystal clarity, without the histrionics and woolly literary allusions that were so popular with famous "pulpiteers" of his time.

Mark Dever, in his chapter commending preaching and preachers, quotes from an interview that the Doctor gave which summarizes neatly both his Welsh background and his medical training:

> I am not and have never been a typical Welsh preacher. I felt that in preaching the first thing that you had to do was to demonstrate to the people that what you were going to do was very relevant and urgently important. The Welsh style of preaching started with a verse and the preacher then told you the connection and analysed the words, but the man of the world did

not know what he was talking about and was not interested. I started with the man whom I wanted to listen, the patient. It was a medical approach really—here is a patient, a person in trouble, an ignorant man who has been to quacks, and so I deal with all that in the introduction. I wanted to get the listener and *then* come to my exposition. They started with their exposition and ended with a bit of application.[6]

Dever makes clear that he himself follows such an expository pattern in his preaching, now nearly four decades since the Doctor spoke these words. It is what makes the Doctor timeless, as of course does all Bible-based exposition, since the fallen condition of humankind never changes.

---

[6] Mark Dever, "What I've Learned about Preaching from Martyn Lloyd-Jones," in Lloyd-Jones, *Preaching and Preachers*, 256.

2

From Wales to
Westminster Chapel

Martyn Lloyd-Jones, twentieth-century expository preacher *par excellence*, was born on December 20, 1899, and died on March 1, 1981. He was not born to wealth or privilege. His father, Henry Lloyd-Jones, was a village storekeeper who later moved to London when his business went bankrupt. His mother, Magdalen Evans, was a farmer's daughter, and Llwyn Cadfor, her family farm in South Wales, was to remain a focal point for the Doctor his entire life. He stayed in touch with the cousins who eventually inherited both the farm and also the successful horse-breeding business based there. One could say that he had his father's considerable intellect— in another age Henry Lloyd-Jones would have gone to university and had a high-flying career—as well as the dynamism of his Evans forebears.

Significantly though, when Martyn was buried in 1981, it was with his *wife's* family, the Phillips. His elder brother Harold, a gifted poet, survived the horrors of the Western Front in World War I only to die in 1918 in the huge influenza epidemic that killed millions worldwide. His younger brother became Sir Vincent Lloyd-Jones, a distinguished High Court judge and a well-known figure in literary and political circles in Wales. Henry Lloyd-Jones, his beloved father, died in 1925. Even decades later, when American Christian thinker Carl Henry asked whether his father was a Christian, Martyn looked tearful, because he simply did not know how to respond.

While in the providence and mercy of God a family can have generations of Christians—as has been the case with the Phillips family—it is not something that can be expected, as the Doctor made clear in, for example, his book *Life in the Spirit*. God can use those from unknown backgrounds, and the Doctor himself is a classic case.

The Doctor liked to say that he was never a teenager in the way that we understand that phase of life today. He nearly died in a fire in his childhood home in Wales, and his father's bankruptcy gave him a sense of responsibility for his family that weighed heavily on him. This—combined with the fact that the Doctor never made jokes in the pulpit—caused some people to think that he was a somber person. In truth his sense of humor was infectious and lifelong, especially when he was with people in his family or close circle of friends with whom he could relax. And when he and his brother Vincent launched into their favorite puns, no one could stay glum.

I think that he was probably a mix of introvert as well as extrovert, which has also been a source of much misunderstanding about him as a person, because, whichever of the two he was, he would put forward his views with tenacious zeal. Outside of family and an inner circle he was a rather shy man, and someone who did not engage in small talk or false bonhomie. He loved to discuss issues not just because he was fascinated with them all his life, but also because that is who he was and what he did. He would do this, when older, around the family table, drawing from his recent reading, from what he had been working on in his sermons, or from the news of the day.

Except for the humor, which was private, and the very profound love and affection he had for his family and close friends, one could say that the public man and the personal were one and the same— his love for debate, for example, and of verbal repartee, were no different in a meeting of ministers than around the intimacy of the family table at mealtimes. He was a man who practiced what he preached in whatever context he found himself. Although he felt one should not laugh about the fate of a lost humanity or show humor from the pulpit, among friends or family he indulged his fabulous sense of humor.

When the family moved to London, lack of money did not prevent the increasingly gifted Martyn from gaining admission to one of London's best schools, St. Marylebone Grammar (the Old Philologian), in the same part of London, Westminster, where he would one day become known around the world.

Soon he was a medical student at a much younger age than usual (sixteen) at St. Bartholomew's Hospital in London, one of the top medical training schools in the country, and one of the oldest. It was joked that "you could always tell a Bart's man and that you could not tell him much." Here he shone, becoming one of their best and brightest students, and at the unusually young age of twenty-one, a full doctor of medicine. He was also Chief Clinical Assistant to the Royal Physician to King George V, Lord Horder, the top diagnostic physician of the day. He would turn down all honorary doctorates on the basis that anyone who had the MD of London University had the best doctorate available and needed no further awards.

Being in London changed his life in other ways too. The Lloyd-Jones family—parents, oldest brother Harold, middle brother Martyn, and youngest brother Vincent—began to attend a Welsh chapel near the famous Charing Cross Road, as did another family, the Phillipses. Thomas Phillips was a highly eminent eye surgeon, with a big house in Harrow and a consulting room in Harley Street. He and his wife, Margaret, had three children—Ieuan, later to become a preacher in South Wales; Bethan, a medical student at Bart's great rival, University College Hospital in London; and Tomas John, later to follow his father as an eye surgeon. Ieuan and Martyn would become lifelong friends—but it was Bethan whom Martyn particularly noticed. Striking and much admired, Bethan was eighteen months older than Martyn, and for many years his feelings for her were unreciprocated. But over the course of time, things changed, and in January 1927 they married, to live, as the famous saying goes, happily ever after.

Today we would call their marriage *complementarian*. But they never used such terminology. She always said that it was her job to keep him in the pulpit. So he preached and she managed the household, a true Proverbs 31 woman of noble character! The point for us today is that they simply got on with a biblical marriage and lifestyle. They never enquired whether she was submitting enough or whether he was leading sufficiently. They studied the Bible together, prayed together, and led the life that any biblical couple should, and with much happiness. She was no doormat! They respected each other for the tasks that God had called the other to fulfill.

Significantly, the Phillips family had played a role in the great revivals in Wales both in 1859 and in 1904. Bethan and her older brother had witnessed much of the latter revival personally, as their father had sent them there to see and experience it for themselves. (He felt that they could catch up on schoolwork but would never have the opportunity to see revival again.) Revival was to be a major preoccupation of the Doctor's life. In 1959, one hundred years after the great awakenings both in the United States and Wales, he would preach one of his most famous sermon series on the subject of revival itself, and how the Bible saw it. He longed to see revival himself. Although he witnessed it on a small scale in parts of his ministry in Wales and believed that Christians should pray for it unceasingly, he would never experience revival on the scale of those great outpourings about which he loved to preach.

Martyn would look back and say that during his early days in medicine, he was not yet a Christian, but that the hound of heaven was after him, convicting him of sin but also working on his conscience in a manner that showed him how man's cures were not God's cures. Many of the Bart's patients were from the top echelons of British society and led lives that were not attractive to behold. The Phillipses knew the prime minister for some of this time, David Lloyd George, a fellow Welshman whose eye doctor was Tomas Phillips. Lloyd George, despite professing Christian faith outwardly, had a young mistress during his time as prime minister. All this Martyn noticed, and found it empty.

In due time the Holy Spirit worked in him in two different ways. First, he was converted to his own true faith in Jesus Christ. But second he realized that while he was mixing with educated and privileged people in London, the poor Welsh folk from whom he had come were living in spiritual darkness.

So at the age of twenty-six he gave up what would have been a very prominent medical career in London, capital not just of Britain but then of the British Empire. He returned to Wales not as a doctor of medicine but as a physician of souls, as a pastor for the Welsh Forward Movement, part of the Welsh Calvinistic Methodist group of his childhood.

This move, coupled with his wedding, was so astonishing that it actually made the national press. The newlyweds went to Sandfields in Aberavon. This was a run-down part of South Wales that, after the Great Depression hit, would become poorer still, with many of the local workers—from the steel works or the docks—out of work and rife with alcoholism. But these were the people in need of the gospel, and to whom the Doctor had been called, and from 1927 to 1938 he had a ministry there that is still spoken of and remembered. Today many evangelicals gravitate to the suburbs. However, the Doctor rejected the suburbs for the industrial poverty of a failing town.

Early in their time in Aberavon, the Lloyd-Joneses celebrated the birth of their elder daughter Elizabeth. Elizabeth's childhood years in such circumstances made an impression that has never left her. With the birth of Ann nearly ten years later, the Lloyd-Jones quartet was completed, giving Martyn the family and emotional security needed as the human base for his God-given ministry, first in Wales and then in London and the world beyond.

What is as significant for us now as it was then is the fact that he treated the congregation with the same intellectual courtesy and respect that he would have given his socially eminent patients in London. He knew, as he would often boast, that the ordinary working men (though often unemployed) could, if taught properly, understand God's truth and biblical theology every bit as well as a university professor. He never throughout his life condescended or dumbed down—something that students from developing countries and also children appreciated in later years, as he treated all of them as intellectual equals, all fully capable of grasping the most complex truths.

The Doctor's approach is wholly biblical—among the writers of the New Testament, only Luke and Paul were educated, and most of the disciples were simple fishermen. Yet it was just such a group of people that turned the world upside down, transformed the Roman Empire, and spread Christianity across the globe.

Lloyd-Jones's *Evangelistic Sermons from Aberavon* reveal his high view of the congregation to which he was preaching. The idea that one had to dumb down the gospel or the message would have been utterly insulting to him. Perhaps because he was not from a university-educated family himself, but one in which learning was much revered, he knew that ordinary people could understand far more than those from middle-class homes gave them credit. This is something that we often forget today.

As Bethan Lloyd-Jones demonstrates in her small book *Memories of Sandfields*, extraordinary things happened in their time in Wales, with the unlikeliest people becoming gloriously saved. This was no seeker-sensitive church. In fact, one of the first things Martyn did was to scrap the choir and to abolish the antidrink Temperance League. Alcoholics did indeed go on to give up their drunken ways, but through being converted and not via well-meaning middle-class good works. To us today this may seem counterintuitive, with all the schemes we have to get people through the church door. But to the Doctor it was a simple case of following the biblical pattern, a theme that will run through this book as it did throughout his life in ministry.

It is interesting that he never formally attended a theological college or seminary. It could be said that he was very much the exception that proves the rule. In those days evangelical seminaries did not exist in Britain such as they do today. One of these he founded himself, the London Theological Seminary. Following Dr. Lloyd-Jones's precepts, this school awards no degrees. It concentrates strongly on the practical rather than on the academic.

The LTS still has students, though today many in Britain go to colleges that do award degrees. One can see the Doctor's ideals and rationale, but one can also wonder whether everyone can enter the ministry in the unique way in which he did.

Over time, Lloyd-Jones's fame spread, even across the Atlantic. He and his wife both loved the United States and spent as many summers there as possible. As he recovered from his first bout with cancer, he delivered his master lectures on preaching to the students of Westminster Theological Seminary. His annual summer in the United States would become a way in which thousands of Americans who were unable to cross the Atlantic themselves could become familiar with his preaching and ministry. Today countless people fondly recall their opportunities to hear the Doctor in person. Many such listeners would become the core of his wide readership in the United States when his books started to be published there as well as in the United Kingdom.

The fact that a preacher from a small industrial town in Wales was invited to speak in the 1930s at some of the major Christian conference venues in the United States shows that he was recognized internationally as a man with something to say. And remember: this was before he went to Westminster Chapel, a much bigger and more famous platform. His preaching power was already making waves across the world.

In 1938 the eminent preacher G. Campbell Morgan asked Lloyd-Jones to become his joint minister at Westminster Chapel, one of the biggest Free Churches in Britain and a place with a global reputation. Largely forgotten today, Morgan was one of the pulpit giants of his time. Leaving his successful ministry in Wales would be a major change for the Doctor.

He decided to accept, and when Morgan retired in 1943, Lloyd-Jones became sole minister of Westminster Chapel, remaining there until cancer forced his retirement in 1968. And although it is for his ministry here that he is best remembered, the Doctor was already well known in Wales and in the United States. One of the themes of this book is that the Doctor was and remains a truly global figure, someone of relevance everywhere. His ministry was already demonstrating exactly that.

3

From Westminster Chapel to the Wider World

Martyn Lloyd-Jones is most famous for his ministry at Westminster Chapel. This was one of the biggest platforms that a non-Anglican in Britain could have. But such was the power of his preaching that he soon became renowned for it not just in Britain but also in the United States and in the world beyond. The Chapel might have been his base, but in reality his ministry was already global, especially after the end of the Second World War, when international travel became safe again.

In Britain we still have a saying that someone is the kind of person who could have survived the Blitz (the bombing of London by Germany in WWII). The Lloyd-Jones family did survive it as well as the subsequent V-1 and V-2 raids, during which they were all in London. Westminster Chapel itself was not hit directly, but was damaged by a large bomb falling a short distance away. Mark Dever quotes the fact that when plaster started to fall from the ceiling of the Chapel when the bomb nearby exploded, the Doctor, who was praying, paused briefly, then continued and afterward preached his full sermon![1] Not even enemy action stopped him from expounding the Bible to his congregation.

What made the Second World War unique was that for the first time civilian casualties far exceeded those of soldiers fighting in the field. London was affected especially badly, with tens of thousands killed or injured. The Doctor's first book *Why Does God Allow War?* (also published as *Why Does God Allow Suffering?*) spoke from Scripture to a congregation upon whom all kinds of horrors were dropping from the air, not just in the first Blitz but throughout the war. The Bible, as he showed in those sermons, had direct relevance to a country facing an existential crisis of the most hideous kind. In hindsight we know the Germans never landed or conquered the nation, but not until the United States entered two years into the war in Europe was Britain truly safe from the barbarity that followed a Nazi invasion.

After the war Lloyd-Jones's congregation grew, with folk coming increasingly from all over the Southeast of England, some from many miles, to attend Westminster Chapel. Many people had to stay all day, arriving in time for the eleven o'clock morning service and not leaving until after the coffee time after the six thirty service, which would have been around eight thirty or later. Temporary wartime lunch facilities became permanent, and hundreds lunched there and then had tea after the afternoon Bible classes (the British equivalent of all-age Sunday school in the United States). The Chapel, while geographically disparate, was a community. This created a unique grouping of people who lived tens of miles and more apart yet for decades would spend Sundays together.

It was of course the Doctor's preaching that drew people in numbers unique for London. Only the ministry of John Stott a few miles away at All Souls Church, Langham Place, came anywhere near the congregational size that Westminster Chapel witnessed in these years. Indeed, some of those listening to the Doctor on Sun-

---

[1] Mark Dever, "What I've Learned about Preaching from Martyn Lloyd-Jones," in Martyn Lloyd-Jones, *Preaching and Preachers*, ed. Kevin DeYoung (Grand Rapids, MI: Zondervan, 2011), 258.

days were young curates from All Souls. Also present was a profoundly impressed young Anglican theologian named James Packer.

This period, Packer was later to recall, was Martyn Lloyd-Jones at his peak of unmatched excellence. Many of these sermons would be published after his death, so that his earlier preaching at the Chapel became widely known *after* those he delivered in later years. His most notable sermons from these early years were those from his series on Ephesians, preached on Sundays, and Romans, preached on Friday evenings.

The Sunday morning sermons were preached to Christians, and the evenings were essentially evangelistic, though as Scripture-based and expository as those in the mornings. Friday nights began as informal discussions, not sermons. It is important to recall that the Doctor would refuse to allow his own sermons or views to be regarded as authoritative. Everything had to be proved from Scripture.

This was a vital principle to Lloyd-Jones. Quoting the Puritans or such eminent nineteenth-century commentators as Warfield was no substitute for the Word of God. For a person's statement to be accurate, it had to be biblical. The importance of this cannot be exaggerated. This principle was at the heart of his saying that he was a "Bible Calvinist not a system Calvinist." In other words, his Calvinism sprung from his interpretation of the Bible, our prime source, rather than from secondary sources such as Calvin's *Institutes* and the great Calvinist writers down the centuries. During his time at the Chapel, he did preach sermons outside of the comfort zone of some of the more systematically Reformed. He did so for the sole reason that he strongly believed that he was simply expounding what the Scriptures taught. This was certainly controversial among some. But it is what he held strongly to be biblical truth. So with his own family and with the attenders of his Friday night talks at the Chapel, agreement *with him* was not a condition of a good relationship, but *argument on the basis of Scripture* was compulsory.

Then he delivered what became his series on Christian doctrines for the Friday nighters. One might presume that because people are Christians, they have an instinctive knowledge of the basics of biblical doctrine. Even in the 1950s it was evident to the Doctor that this was not the case. In our own time it is even more vital to understand this, as those converted from non-Christian backgrounds often do not have the remotest grasp of what Christians believe and why. Discipleship, the Doctor realized, was a vital necessity, and his series on Christian doctrine probably teaches more theology than many a seminary course.

Some of the great sermons he gave during this period are also examples of apologetics, in the right sense of the term. If one's preaching is Bible-based, there should be no clash between apologetics and exposition. This is because apologetics flows naturally from the truth of God as seen in Scripture as well as from the world that God has made, which we see around us. The sermons that he preached at Wheaton College in the United States, which later turned into his book *Truth Unchanged, Unchanging*, are good examples of this genre.

It is interesting to note that it was at the same time that the Doctor was preaching this particular series that Francis Schaeffer was experiencing a profound discovery of what was implied by *truth*. In Schaeffer's case, this renewed understanding resulted in his concept of *true truth* and the founding of the L'Abri Fellowship. Not long after, the Doctor and Schaeffer met for the first time. While the Doctor was wary of apologetics outside of the context of expository preaching, many would now argue that there was less difference between the two men than some have supposed. Their methods might have been different, but their Christ-centered goals were the same.

Dr. Lloyd-Jones, while always professing himself closer to the great eighteenth-century preachers such as Jonathan Edwards, was nonetheless in this period also instrumental in reviving evangelical interest in the great Puritan theologians and thinkers of the past, such as John Owen. His talks were always the high point at annual conferences, and until 1966, his participation in such conferences was always done in collaboration with J. I. Packer, who was by then a leading authority on Puritan theology. In addition the Doctor strongly backed the foundation of the Banner of Truth Trust, to reprint important volumes from the past. Iain Murray, its founder, spent some years on the staff of Westminster Chapel during the Banner's early days.

When it came to the Doctor's preaching, his hallmark high view of preaching from Scripture influenced all that he did, week by week. By the 1950s he was preaching three sermons a week: two on Sunday and one on Friday. His view also made a major difference to his evangelism, and to style as well as substance. Do we play down the offense of the cross in order not to sound too harsh? Do we use music to make non-Christians comfortable in a church environment? Such practices were utterly abhorrent to the Doctor.

Some of his views on the work and ministry of the Holy Spirit would become controversial. But anyone who, like Dr. Lloyd-Jones, believes in the doctrines of grace knows full well the power of the Holy Spirit to convict and to convert. If one *truly* believes in such doctrines, and, to use a modern expression, if one is genuinely *Reformed* as well as restless, then man-made gimmicks should surely be as anathema today as they were to the Doctor in his thirty years in the pulpit of Westminster Chapel. His preaching there reflected what he believed, and his theory and practice tied in well together.

Tim Keller was to find this especially important in assessing the ministry and preaching style of Dr. Lloyd-Jones. It is important, Keller notes, that Dr. Lloyd-Jones did not presume that everyone listening to him was a Christian, even though the sermons were geared for believers in the morning and unbelievers at night.

Around this time the Doctor became the first chairman of the executive committee of the International Fellowship of Evangelical Students (IFES), of which he later became the president. IFES was truly global and indeed is more so today than ever, since areas of the world where the gospel was forbidden or unknown are now some of the strongest evangelical regions of the twenty-first century.

Studies that concentrate on Lloyd-Jones as a British figure sadly omit this vital part of his international life and ministry, which was central to his life for well over a quarter of a century. The fact that IFES began as strongly evangelical as it did after World War II is very much a result of his influence and Bible-centered thinking. While this book concentrates on the Doctor as a preacher, one cannot fully appreciate him without considering this crucial ministry.

THE DOCTOR'S SERMON SERIES

In 1950 he began what still remains one of his best-known sermon series, that on the Sermon on the Mount. Even in nonevangelical circles, these expositions are internationally famous and are often the only Lloyd-Jones books that pastors of a different theological persuasion possess by him. It is of course a series on some of Christ's most basic teaching, and his series conclusion remains a classic. This was the period when he was gaining fame as an expositor both at home and overseas (especially in the United States, where he continued to love to visit and to preach whenever possible).

The Sermon on the Mount series was intelligent, reasoned, Scripture-based, and timeless. It was delivered with passion and total conviction, in great contrast to the popular pulpit fillers of his own generation in London, most of whom now lie forgotten, their works dated, and their theologies—if they had any—long since discredited.

What is extraordinary among many things about the Doctor during this period is the scale of his preaching. Those three sermons a week were a far heavier workload than most pastors would ever want to take on, yet there he was, in his late fifties, on a schedule that many a preacher in their twenties or thirties would find exhausting. It was, his family maintains, his dependence upon the power of the Holy Spirit—his view of unction being at the heart of all his preaching—that kept him going.

And we must remember that at this time he was also a guest preacher in other parts of Britain, sometimes to audiences of thousands, as well as overseas and often in the United States in his summer holidays. Here too he preached instead of slept. Not until the 1960s would he have holidays in Balsham in Cambridgeshire, but even then much of his time was taken up preparing earlier sermon series for publication. His duties with IFES was another major time commitment, along with those conferences, especially on the Puritans, for which his annual lecture was the main concluding event.

Yet in no sense was he ever a workaholic. He had the strong self-discipline to pace himself, to take a break when necessary, and to be a pastor to those who looked to him for guidance. For such people, for close friends and family, he was always available, to their profound joy and gratitude.

In a rare vignette concerning his inspiration for preaching, Dr. Lloyd-Jones tells the story of how *Spiritual Depression: Its Causes and Cure* was conceived. While he was getting dressed one morning, he was suddenly overwhelmed by the Spirit of God to preach a series on spiritual depression rather than on Ephesians, as he had planned.

> Quite literally while I was dressing the series took order in my mind and all various texts, and the order in which they had come to me, in that way. I had never thought about preaching a series of sermons on spiritual depression. . . . I always pay great attention to such happenings.[2]

The Doctor was a doctor in more senses than one—both medical and spiritual—and in the case of his congregation, and that of the Westminster Fellowship of Ministers, he was both. With his acute medical knowledge—which he kept up all his life, reading medical journals for fun to the end of his days—and with his pastor's insights, he could see how a member of the Chapel congregation or a struggling preacher might be run down and depressed *physically* and *mentally* and therefore be more open to *spiritual* attack. And while sin sometimes caused spiritual dryness or isolation, it could

---

[2] Lloyd-Jones, *Preaching and Preachers*, 203.

be that, as with Job, Satan was attacking a faithful and innocent child of God. Maybe God was testing one of his own children for his or her particular good.

As a medically trained physician with a deep understanding of human psychology, as well as a pastor charged by God with the spiritual care of souls, the Doctor knew that the permutations of sin, frailty, and the human psyche were many and various. He was both pastor and teacher to his congregation.

And so *Spiritual Depression*, perhaps his best-selling book ever, is still in print and read as much six decades after it was first conceived. It has helped millions of Christians—thanks in many ways to the enthusiastic support of George Verwer of Operation Mobilisation, whose passionate advocacy of it worldwide has made it probably the most used of all the Doctor's works.

The chapter entitled "Heart, Mind, and Will" shows the Doctor to be both an outstanding biblical expositor and one who continued to be influenced by the medical training God had put him through in the 1920s. True biblical preaching appeals to the heart (our emotions), to our mind (our intellect), and to our will (we do something as a result of it). This unique combination was at the heart of all of his preaching—the *logic on fire* and its application with the employment of our will. This was so unlike the preaching of his time, which usually appealed to either heart or head, but seldom to both, and which never appealed to the human will to implement what was learned in everyday life.

What was true in the 1950s remains the same in our own time. Cerebral sermons, emotionally excessive and manipulative sermons, and no application of what kind of life should be lived on Monday morning are empty, ephemeral, and ultimately meaningless. The importance of the Doctor's very different combination cannot be emphasized enough, since this particular combination—*heart, mind, and will*—is as important, in many ways, as his actual words. Many a preacher today would do well to emulate such an approach and to encourage his congregation through it. While we can grasp that sermons should be Bible-based and Christ-centered, preaching with unction—of the kind that appeals to heart, mind, and will—is not so common. As the Doctor liked to put it, even a beautiful graveyard is lifeless.

In the evangelical world, he is best known for his epic expository sermons, in particular, as we have seen, his series on Ephesians and on Romans. He spent eight years slowly going through Ephesians, and when he retired in 1968, he edited many of the sermons himself before his death in 1981.

His smaller sermon series have been less well known. But now most of these too have been published. *The Cross*, his evangelistic sermons delivered in 1963, is today among the favorites of many. Preached on Sunday nights over several decades, his final great series of sermons was on *The Acts of the Apostles*, ending finally in 1968.

THE DOCTOR AND CONTROVERSY

In 1966 an Evangelical Alliance meeting took place in London that caused much controversy. The Doctor made his views public on whether evangelicals should stay within doctrinally mixed denominations. This is now often referred to simply as "1966" and was a major turning point in Britain on how the Doctor's ministry was regarded.

We will look at this event in more detail in chapter 6. For now, it is important to say that though this might have made a difference to the Doctor *in Britain*, in the United States and in the wider world people did not change their opinion of him much at all. As his sermons were beginning to be read globally, one could argue that *globally* and especially in the United States his influence was greater than ever before. Many regretted the split with J. I. Packer, who remained within the Church of England. But Packer himself remained a close friend of many of the Doctor's family. Similarly, the Doctor continued to have Anglican friends, such as Philip Edgcumbe Hughes and John Gwyn-Thomas, a contemporary of

Packer's at theological college and later vicar of one of the best-known churches in Cambridge.

But it is perhaps true to say that evangelicals in Britain today have reached a different ecclesiastical configuration to meet the changing needs of the spiritual climate. We have to be faithful to God for how he calls us for our *own* generation, and it is now nearly half a century since the Doctor made his 1966 address. Movements or groups such as Affinity, the Proclamation Trust, Word Alive, and the Evangelical Ministry Assembly in Britain, and Together for the Gospel and The Gospel Coalition in the United States, show how faithful evangelicals are working out ways in which to proclaim the same eternal gospel truths in our own generation. Indeed in 2014 the Proclamation Trust heard a talk by Vaughan Roberts, the Rector of St. Ebbe's, the major evangelical and Anglican church in Oxford, emphasizing the need to continue in the paths once trod by Martyn Lloyd-Jones. The effects of 1966 are now increasingly becoming part of history, and no longer define how the Doctor is perceived. (The chapter on this issue in the book edited by Andrew Atherstone, *Engaging with Martyn Lloyd-Jones*, is particularly good, especially for those seeking an objective account.[3])

Another controversy came from the series that the Doctor preached in Westminster Chapel in the early 1960s on the first chapter of the Gospel of John, in particular verses 26 and 33, on baptism with the Holy Spirit.

Enormous amounts of ink have been spilled on his views; the chapter in *Engaging with Martyn Lloyd-Jones* is a model of objectivity and fully researched analysis. (We will explore this topic further in chap. 4.)

The Doctor, in endeavoring to give what he felt to be a correct biblical exegesis of a much-debated issue, had a position that was neither cessationist nor Pentecostal. Because of his iconic status among many evangelicals, however, those on *both* sides of the divide, especially within the Reformed constituency, claimed him as

---

[3] Andrew Atherstone, "Lloyd-Jones and the Anglican Secession Crisis," in *Engaging with Martyn Lloyd-Jones: The Life and Legacy of "The Doctor"* (Nottingham: Apollos, 2011), 261–92.

their own. But he believed (1) in the continuation of the sign gifts and in the baptism with the Holy Spirit as a postconversion experience but that (2) God chose who received what gift and that the "baptism with the Holy Spirit" was something God gave for a purpose, not as a status for life.

This meant that he had sympathies *in effect* for both sides and neither, so that attempts by both Pentecostals and cessationists to lay exclusive claim to him were in reality impossible. Attempts by well-meaning enthusiasts on each side have been made, but if one looks at him as someone who simply believed in the faithful exposition of Scripture, such efforts, however well intentioned, are surely futile. You may not like what he said, but to insist that what he *really* meant was something quite different, utterly fails to understand his whole biblical mind-set. As we saw earlier, he always insisted he was a "Bible Calvinist not a system Calvinist." Of fewer issues is that more true than what he actually believed on how Scripture views the baptism and gifts of the Holy Spirit.

One of the main points of our book is that you do not have to agree with the Doctor in terms of his *conclusions*. However, it is wise to employ his *method*, which is that all doctrine and practice should originate in Scripture. This is why we look at his exposition of this topic under the heading of *sola scriptura*, the Reformation principle of Scripture alone—rather than under the headline of charismatic gifts. *How* he arrived at his conclusions is as important as *where* he ended up.

THE DOCTOR'S INFLUENTIAL LATER YEARS

In 1968 the Doctor developed cancer, from which he fully recovered. But he felt that it was a call from God to embark upon a wider ministry.

Some of the causes in which he became involved were based in Britain and have been well described, from works by Iain Murray to the *Engaging with Martyn Lloyd-Jones* symposium edited by Atherstone, that is such a useful guide to his life. The Evangelical

Movement of Wales, the Evangelical Library in London, the FIEC, and the London Theological Seminary all received much attention and encouragement from him during this final phase of his ministry. As they are so well written about elsewhere, we do not need to focus on them here. And a caveat: these are *British* activities, undertaken just at a time when his fame and influence became truly global. He had been revered for decades in the United States and in parts of the world where those who knew him through IFES were able to spread the word of his many God-given talents and abilities.

As previously noted, while his influence *in Britain* post-1966 was diminished, as his circle of followers was smaller, this was certainly not true on a *global* perspective. If anything it grew much wider, and not just because he was able to go abroad and preach more easily. In the United States he was reaching more people than ever.

He was now able to spend more time editing his sermons for publication. When in Cambridgeshire staying with family, his calls could be screened, and he could sit down and concentrate upon the task at hand. His books from this time became international best-sellers and brought him to the attention of people worldwide who could never have made it to Britain to hear him preach in person. His works were translated into dozens of languages and were sold on many continents, from Asia to Latin America, and through this means he gained a constituency far larger than any he had enjoyed before.

This created a momentum such that his books, with the new global readership, continued to sell after his death, and in larger numbers than in his lifetime. As the biblical expression goes, he being dead still speaks.

Much of his time was also spent as a pastor's pastor, and in particular with those who had heeded his call in 1966 to withdraw from doctrinally mixed denominations into groups such as the FIEC. He felt a strong sense of responsibility for such preachers, and he would both preach for them in person in their churches and give them his sage advice on the telephone. His annual talks to groups such as the Puritan Conference continued, and were as appreciated as ever.

We should therefore reassess the view (which some people hold) that 1968–1981, from his retirement from the Chapel to his death on March 1, 1981, was one of decline. There is proof that it was the exact opposite! For Christians in places such as Brazil, Korea, and the United States, the battles in Britain were either unknown or of no relevance to their own lives and ministry. What mattered was that through reading his works translated into their own language and through hearing him at conferences, they could appreciate this prince of preachers for themselves, and in the case of millions of new readers, for the first time. This renaissance of interest in the Doctor and in his views and sermons has perhaps even increased, so that he is more known worldwide today than he ever was when alive.

He died, rather appropriately, on Sunday, March 1, 1981. Sunday is the Lord's Day, and March 1 is the national day of Wales, his home country. He became ill in 1980, and as he lay dying in February 1981, he told his family not to pray for healing and not to hold him back from the glory. God answered his request. His burial service was in Wales, in the graveyard of his wife's family, the Phillipses, a place redolent of Christian history and of the great Welsh Revival in his youth. The memorial service in Westminster Chapel was packed, with thousands present. But, as we have seen, his voice was not silenced; the impact of his ministry continues to this day.

4

Just Say Biblical

MARTYN LLOYD-JONES AND THE
CENTRALITY OF SCRIPTURE

Many years ago Bethan Lloyd-Jones, then the Doctor's widow, said to a group of listeners, "Why do people use all these names? Why can't they just say biblical?"

If only!

One of the greatest divides that we have in the Christian church today is exactly what the term *biblical* really entails. Of course, we always say that what we believe is scriptural.

Or do we?

In his biography of John MacArthur, Iain Murray quotes his subject as disliking labels—such as *Reformed* or *Calvinist*—preferring instead to base his views on the teaching of the Bible. Murray correctly states that Martyn Lloyd-Jones had the same outlook.[1]

In his famous Friday night discussions at Westminster Chapel, which took place before his great expository series Great Doctrines and then Romans, Dr. Lloyd-Jones led his congregation in a debate on what Christians should believe and why. Discussion

---

[1] Iain Murray, *John MacArthur* (Edinburgh: Banner of Truth, 2011), 206–7.

often ranged widely! A young trainee accountant named Frederick Catherwood, his future son-in-law, often found himself the foil of the Doctor, since he was one of the brave few never afraid to answer back!

There was one absolute rule though. *All* responses had to be *Bible-based*. No human authority was allowed. The *Westminster Confession* might say it, the *Heidelberg Catechism* might be quite clear on it, and the Doctor himself might have preached on the issue only the week before, but however powerful or historic the source, it had to be backed by clear reference to Scripture.

Often the Doctor would push people on the logic of their conclusions. The fallacy or hopelessness or misguided nature or shaky ground of their beliefs or arguments would be exposed—all very lovingly and pastorally, but revealed nonetheless. (Os Guinness has pointed out in lectures as well as in print that Francis Schaeffer was similar in one-on-one evangelism; he would also employ Scripture as the ultimate source of truth.)

The Doctor also enjoyed debate within his family. One of the things he loved to do over the kitchen table in the Catherwood household near Cambridge was to stir up discussion among his own descendants. Here he would sometimes play devil's advocate, arguing zealously for a position he did not himself hold, but to which he felt we needed to respond. Grandchildren sometimes go where adults fear to tread, and we could be quite animated in debate. But the same rules applied. Our positions had to be *biblical* rather than just good ideas or debating points. *Why* did we believe what we believed?

The magisterial Reformers had a phrase for this: *sola scriptura*, which means "Scripture alone." The Roman Catholic Church had two sources of final authority—as it still does: Scripture and the tradition of the Church. One of the greatest Reformation achievements was to abolish the latter and declare that only the former, the Word of God as delivered in Scripture, was of complete and incontestable authority within God's people, the church. The apostle Paul himself confirms this when he says that even if he or an angel from heaven contradicts God's Word, such denial is anathema and false, since *only* the Word of God, the Bible, is true (Gal. 1:8).

Of course, as anyone can observe, Protestants have countless denominations. Dr. Lloyd-Jones loved going to Scotland, among other places, for his holidays. As he well knew, the history of Reformed Christianity in that country is one of endless splits and counter-splits, and sometimes splits from reunions from original splits. Of the making of Presbyterian denominations, let alone of others, there seems no end.

This happens because, although we all in theory agree that Scripture alone is the final authority, in practice we interpret in often divergent ways what Luther once described as *matters indifferent*. Bible-believing evangelicals may be united on the core of the faith, but have differing views on issues from baptism to church government to pacifism to the order of events by which people come to salvation. We thus have Baptists, Presbyterians, Methodists, and Pentecostals all in full accord with the heart of the gospel, the work of Jesus Christ upon the cross, but having a wide variety of views on other matters.

Martyn Lloyd-Jones actually did believe in *sola scriptura*. This might seem an odd comment to make, as it would seem plainly obvious that so outstanding an evangelical leader would hold zealously to such an important doctrine! But the point is that he *really* believed it. The principle of *sola scriptura* made a complete difference to his life and ministry and to how he approached every issue with which he dealt. The "whole problem"—to use words that he would often employ in his evangelistic sermons—is that as evangelicals we often assent to this principle in *theory* but not *in practice*. Dr. Lloyd Jones, however, held to the twin facets of intellectual agreement and practical outworking.

He has sometimes been called the last of the towering Welsh Calvinistic Methodists, the denomination into which he was born. Looking at it logically, the idea of being both a Calvinist and a

Methodist is ludicrous! It is perhaps an achievement uniquely Welsh. But consider two things.

First, Calvin and Wesley may have disagreed on some doctrines that were not unimportant. But on the core understanding of Christ upon the cross and salvation through Christ alone, both men would be in full agreement

Second, think of how Martyn Lloyd-Jones defined preaching: *logic on fire; theology coming through a man who is on fire.* He had, countless people have accurately suggested, the logic of Calvin coupled with the fire of the eighteenth-century Methodist revival. His preaching, logical and filled with unction, speaking with biblical authority and in the power of the Holy Spirit, embodied the best of the two approaches.

Many people have tried to claim Dr. Lloyd-Jones for themselves. In recent years they have done so in opposite directions! He has alas become a football kicked by warring factions within the evangelical fold. How has this happened? And to which of his views has this most occurred—and why? And why has this chapter given over a thousand words of context before addressing two of the Doctor's most controversial opinions: on the baptism and gifts of the Holy Spirit and on the nature of the church?

First, he began everything with what the Bible taught. Second, this is how he wished his congregation, his family, and his readers to think. If you believe X, then prove X from Scripture.

Third, one wonders how much we as supposedly Bible-believing, *sola scriptura* holding evangelicals follow that tenet *in practice* as he did. (We can hopefully take for granted that most readers of this book will do so in theory!)

What determines our belief? We must remember it is *sola* scriptura, Scripture *alone*. How much does our denomination influence us? Is it the Bible or is it the views of our favorites from church history that shape our thinking?

Some years ago distinguished American Southern Baptist R. T. Kendall wrote a book that discussed whether one of Calvin's "five points" was in fact the invention of some of his English followers. Not surprisingly, a storm followed! But much of the argument that followed was depressingly on the grounds that as the five points were true, Calvin *must* therefore have believed them himself! And so the debate that then raged was on whether Calvin was a five-point Calvinist. The discussion should have focused on what Scripture itself actually taught rather than debate the correct interpretation of the works of the great John Calvin.

Surely such a discussion is the Reformed equivalent of medieval scholastics debating how many angels could dance on the head of a pin! If one understands Dr. Lloyd-Jones correctly—and no one was more a fan of historical biography than he was—then the primary question to ask is, *What does Scripture say?* No one was a greater enthusiast for church history than the Doctor himself. He would astonish his daughters by sitting, fully clothed and wearing a hat, shoes, and socks, on the beach. While other fathers were in shorts swimming, making sand castles, or playing beach cricket, the Doctor would be immersed in the Puritans, devouring seventeenth-century theology in the way that the other fathers near him would devour ice cream! But his approach to all controversy was to consider whether the Bible—not historical figures—actually teaches the doctrine in question.

THE DOCTRINES OF GRACE

Not everyone, even adherents of Reformed theology, believe that there is a genuine resurgence in Puritan and Calvinist theology among young people, with university students reading the works of Jonathan Edwards with the enthusiasm of a Martyn Lloyd-Jones on a Welsh beach eighty years ago.

But *something* is happening. People such as Mark Dever, Al Mohler, D. A. Carson, Tim Keller, and John Piper are leading a resurgence of interest in Reformed theology similar to the way in which Martyn Lloyd-Jones did back in the 1940s.

And interestingly, many of the people I have just named are

Baptists. This is one of the many exciting things about the gatherings in the United States such as The Gospel Coalition and Together for the Gospel. Baptists, Presbyterians, and what one can describe as Reformed charismatics come together under one roof, so to speak. All these denominationally separate groups are united in their common allegiance to the gospel and to a Reformed understanding of what are called the doctrines of grace.

Logically speaking it should be impossible to be Reformed or Calvinist while at the same time being Baptist. Calvin was many things, but he was a firm paedobaptist all his life, as are Presbyterians and Episcopalians/Anglicans to this day. But increasingly the world is full of Baptists who hold zealously to the classic Reformed doctrines of what the theologians call *soteriology*, the way in which salvation is studied and understood. In the United States in particular, the growth of Baptists with strong belief in the doctrines of grace, both inside and outside the Southern Baptist world, has been an exponential one.

So we started with Welsh Calvinistic Methodists, and now we have Calvinistic Baptists. To be fair, both have reputable eighteenth-century precedents. Some of the earliest Baptists as far back as the seventeenth century, known as Particular Baptists, were both Reformed and Baptist—although that historical fact is hotly contested by some Free Will or Arminian Baptists who wish to read their present theology back into the past.

As Iain Murray is so right to point out both in relation to Dr. Lloyd-Jones and John MacArthur, labels can be misleading, and both of these men were and are understandably wary of them.

However, if like Lloyd-Jones or MacArthur, you take your guidance from Scripture alone, rather than from man-made creedal constructions, however wonderful, then this is not a problem. Many evangelicals in Britain and the United States today believe that (1) Scripture teaches that baptism by immersion is a public declaration of *having become* a Christian, and (2) the doctrines of grace are simply a way of encapsulating evident teaching in the Bible of how salvation happens. While a man-centered denominational view sees these two things as being historically separate, you can hold two doctrines that much of history and human wisdom say are incompatible if you believe that *the Bible teaches them.*

This is why Dr. Lloyd-Jones was so difficult to label! People could not fit him into a narrow systematic/denominational groove.

For example, Spurgeon, the towering expositor of nineteenth-century Britain, is justifiably a role model for countless evangelicals today.[2] But Spurgeon rejected Calvin's teaching on baptism! Does this horrify us? Or does it simply show that both Calvin and Spurgeon based all their thought and preaching on how each one interpreted God's Word in the Bible? On the doctrines of grace they agreed fully, and on that of baptism (infants vs. believers only), they interpreted the Scriptures in completely different ways.

So today evangelicalism's cutting edge is populated with Bible-believing Christians who are frequently both Baptist and Calvinist at the same time, even though there are major doctrinal differences (e.g., baptism, church/state relations) between what one can call Spurgeonites—for want of a better term—and Calvinists. Of course many Baptists, both in Britain and in the United States, reject the doctrines of grace completely, but are theologically conservative evangelicals in all other respects. And there are a number of equally doctrinally strict evangelical Presbyterians who would argue that you cannot be genuinely Reformed if you reject the view of Calvin and other magisterial Reformers of the sixteenth century on the issue of baptism.

Martyn Lloyd-Jones's distrust of labels and his wife's famous words, "Why can't they just say biblical?" are surely now making more sense. For now we seem to have four categories:

1. Baptists who say that as their denomination was historically Arminian or Free Will, *real* Baptists reject Reformed theology.

---

[2] The website Grace to You (gty.org) is a twenty-first-century example. On the history of the Puritans see Phillip R. Johnson, "The Hall of Church History: The Puritans," accessed September 14, 2014, http://www.spurgeon.org/~phil/puritans.htm.

2. Baptists who say that as the doctrines of grace are all found in Scripture, belief in them and in their denomination's interpretation of the Bible are thus fully compatible.
3. Presbyterians who agree with Calvin on both these issues but whose wish to have gospel-centered fellowship with Baptists is more important than genuine denominational and interpretation issues—and who think how wonderful it is that such people have come to love the doctrines of grace!
4. Presbyterians who feel that as Baptists, by definition, reject Calvin and many of the great seventeenth-century creeds, they cannot possibly be identified as *Reformed*.

Today British and American evangelicals are putting gospel loyalty ahead of man-made divisions. What is significant about the new movements is that they affirm their common beliefs without pretending that their differences do not exist. This is where true Bible-based affiliations are so different from human attempts at "ecumenism," with one group pretending that a form of words says one thing and another that the same words mean something totally different. (Dr. Lloyd-Jones was particularly scornful of the ecumenical movement for this very reason—in addition to its doctrinal flabbiness, its unity was fundamentally dishonest and based upon pretense.)

The Baptists and Presbyterians coming together in gospel unity do not pretend to agree with each other on everything. But evangelical Baptists discover that with their loyalty to *sola scriptura*, they and similar evangelicals in Presbyterian denominations hold more in common with each other in God's Word than interpretations of secondary doctrines that push them apart.

I have deliberately taken the issue of baptism, in which there is no controversy in relation to him and his teaching, in order to set the foundation for discussion on two issues where there was immense disagreement among his followers: baptism or sealing with the Holy Spirit and the nature and structure of the church.

To pursue this discussion, in the 1980s, during the conservative resurgence in the Southern Baptist Convention, there was much argument on where particular Southern Baptists of earlier days stood. If X, who lived in the early nineteenth century were still alive, what would he be thinking in, say, 1985? And rather like the issue on whether Calvin believed in all of his five points, it was an entirely man-centered argument. Baptist heroes trumped the writers of the Gospels and Epistles, and Baptist history was more important than the Bible. And the conservative victory has not altered this approach, since evangelicals are still appealing to Baptist history and to creedal statements. The champions of the Reformed awakening in the SBC have had to affirm their allegiance to the official Baptist Faith and Message, not in relation to liberals who would deny Scripture, but to fellow evangelicals in the denomination for whom Reformed theology is an abhorrence. (I am indeed simplifying complex issues! But we are looking at it in the context of *sola scriptura* and the twenty-first-century relevance of Martyn Lloyd-Jones.)

In 1971 Martyn Lloyd-Jones addressed a group of IFES students and staff from across the world, in a castle in Austria. All of us present remember the three talks that he gave, entitled "What Is an Evangelical?" (now published in the book *Knowing the Times*). His views on the Bible, as expressed in these talks to the IFES, cannot be clearer.

> What, then, is to be our method in defining what an Evangelical is? The method of course, is primarily Biblical. The great slogan of the Reformation, *sola scriptura*, has always been the slogan of the true Evangelical. The Evangelical starts with the Bible. He is a man of the Book. This is his only authority and he submits himself in everything to this.[3]

He went on to remind his audience in the third lecture, having quoted from the IFES basis of faith that he had helped to draw up some twenty-five years earlier: "Scripture is our *sole* authority . . . our only authority."

---

[3] Martyn Lloyd-Jones, "What Is an Evangelical?," in *Knowing the Times: Addresses Delivered on Various Occasions, 1942–1977* (Edinburgh: Banner of Truth, 1989), 318.

In basing his entire outlook on the Bible—something Iain Murray affirmed in his own writings—Martyn Lloyd-Jones was thus acting as any evangelical should, but he was also ahead of his time.

This is not to say that he belittled history—far from it! The Puritan Conference, the group he set up with J. I. Packer that became the Westminster Conference after their parting of ways in the 1960s, was based on a close study and examination of history. Dr. Lloyd-Jones devoured history! Christians who do not understand the lessons of history are doomed to repeat the mistakes of the past. And the way in which God's people have withstood persecution and suffering since the church began was a source of endless encouragement to him, just as it is to Christians today who read about such things.

The Doctor was fully aware of all the great Reformation creeds and statements of faith, many copies of which he possessed in his own library. Anyone today reading his sermons knows the extent to which he loved to quote from the works of giants of the faith and of the ways in which they formulated their faith.

Nonetheless, Scripture retained its primacy.

Many of those who disagreed with him did so on the grounds of history, and of the great Reformation creeds and formulae. For certain, the magisterial Reformers were not believers in what we now call the "sign gifts." But then Zwingli, whose views on the nature of communion many of us hold today, also had Baptists drowned because of their theology on baptism!

In "What Is an Evangelical?" the Doctor addresses many of the issues upon which evangelicals divide—baptism, church government, the millennium, even the doctrines of grace:

> Now I am a Calvinist; I believe in election and predestination;
> but I would not dream of putting it under the heading of essen-
> tial. I put it under the heading of non-essential. . . . And here,
> while I myself hold very definite and strong views on the subject,
> I will not separate from a man who cannot accept and believe
> in the doctrines of election and predestation, and is Armin-

ian, so long as he tells me that we are all saved by grace, and as long as the Calvinist agrees, as he must, that God calls all men everywhere to repentance. As long as both are prepared to agree about these things I say we must not break fellowship. So I put election into the category of non-essentials.[4]

Spurgeon, who believed more or less the same, could not have put it better! Of course, most readers of this book probably believe in the doctrines of grace themselves, but we have no less than Martyn Lloyd-Jones reminding us that our Arminian brothers and sisters in Christ can be our fellow evangelicals as well.

What is significant is how he categorized the charismatic gifts. He was, in these IFES talks, wary of those who claimed any kind of spiritual superiority on the basis of having received them. He was also most critical of those who put experience above Scripture, and named names in his address. But on the actual principle of belief in the gifts themselves, he told his IFES audience:

> I would put in the same category the whole question of the baptism of the Spirit and the *charismata*, the spiritual gifts. There are differences of opinion here. I regard these as very important, but I would not venture to put them into the category of the essential.[5]

The meaning of those words is surely clear! Evangelicals should not divide on the issue of the baptism of the Holy Spirit, and those on both sides are, if they are right on the doctrines of salvation and of Scripture, evangelical. These lectures are contained in a book published posthumously in 1989, *Knowing the Times*, some years after the controversy of the Doctor's beliefs on this contentious issue.

Let us go on to look at some specifics, being careful to choose, where possible, books he edited in his own lifetime.

In his major series on Ephesians, he makes his own views on

[4] Ibid., 352.
[5] Ibid., 354.

Scripture very clear in the volume entitled *The Christian Soldier: An Exposition of Ephesians 6:10–20*. Interestingly, he expounds his views on the Bible not just in relation to the obvious passage on the "sword of the Spirit" (v. 17) but also in dealing with verse 14, on girding up our loins with truth. Truth as he understood it was Scripture-based, and so the defense of the Bible was as much part of the earlier verse as the more famous part of the Christian armor, the sword of the Spirit. The belt of truth was the *defensive* part of scriptural truth, the sword the *offensive*; but the centrality of Scripture applied equally to both

We cannot reproduce the full chapter here. But as Dr. Martyn Lloyd-Jones said:

> [The] Protestant position, as was the position of the early church in the first centuries, is that the Bible is the Word of God. Not that it "contains" it, but that it is the Word of God, uniquely inspired and inerrant.[6]

(When he was writing this in 1977, Francis Schaeffer was making similar statements in defense of the absolute authority of the Bible—two giants of twentieth-century evangelicalism fighting for the all-sufficiency of Scripture at the same time.[7])

This, the Doctor realized, had pastoral as well as theological implications. He tells us:

> I am concerned . . . not only from the standpoint of the Church in general, but also from the standpoint of our own individual experiences. How can we fight the devil? How can we know how we are to live? . . . Where can I find this truth that I must gird on, as I put on all this armour of God? Where can I find it if I cannot find it in the Bible? . . .
>
> That is the whole Biblical position. In our inability, in our finite condition, in our sinfulness, we cannot, and we never shall

---

[6] Martyn Lloyd-Jones, *The Christian Soldier: An Exposition of Ephesians 6:10–20* (Edinburgh: Banner of Truth, 1977), 211.

[7] See Francis A. Schaeffer, *Two Contents, Two Realities* in *25 Basic Bible Studies* (Wheaton, IL: Crossway, 1996) for a written version of his speech at Lausanne 1974. See also *The Great Evangelical Disaster* (Wheaton, IL: Crossway, 1984).

be able to arrive at a knowledge of God. . . . But, says the Bible, God has done this very thing! That is the whole glory of the message, that is the good news of the Gospel of salvation; God has been pleased to give us this revelation. . . . It is not of men, it is not human literature, its source is divine. . . . The truth is the girdle which you have to put on around your loins.[8]

So the Bible is unique and supremely authoritative.

SOLA SCRIPTURA AND THE BAPTISM OF THE HOLY SPIRIT

Thus with our ground rules in place, we can now look at the Doctor's view of the baptism, or the sealing, of the Holy Spirit, since we now have the right context in which to do so.

Our quotations are deliberately taken from his book *The Sons of God*, which is an exposition of Romans 8:5–17. We will focus on the chapter on Romans 8:16: "The Spirit himself bears witness with our spirit that we are children of God." This was a book published in his lifetime, in 1973 by the Banner of Truth in the United Kingdom and then in the United States. The Doctor himself edited the text, and his publishers fully approved it!

At the time when he was preparing these sermons on Romans 8, he told me personally of his views on this subject. I called him at one o'clock in the morning from a telephone booth in Oxford, from a spot that was just feet away from where great Protestant martyrs such as Nicholas Ridley and Hugh Latimer had been burned at the stake for their beliefs during the reign of Queen Mary in the sixteenth century. That evening I had heard tongues being used for the first time ever, by charismatic students later closely involved with the ministry of the late David Watson, a leading evangelist in the 1970s.

Memory of oral conversations can be unreliable. But what he said to me on the phone is identical to what he wrote in his volume

---

[8] Lloyd-Jones, *Christian Soldier*, 212, 216–17.

on Romans. This fact is important to remember, particularly when evaluating what Dr. Lloyd-Jones did or did not say on this controversial issue. Some writers and speakers are happy to confess that they understand fully what the Doctor wrote, but that they differ in their interpretation of Scripture. John MacArthur and Vaughan Roberts said this publicly, and it is a fair and just position.

But other writers have maintained that they recall conversations in which the Doctor told them of his "real" views! According to one writer, Dr. Lloyd-Jones was a cessationist (like the author himself), and with another, the Doctor's views matched closely with charismatic/Pentecostal theology (again, like that author himself). Since these views, based on recollections of conversations held decades ago, contradict each other entirely, we *might* have a problem! But in fact we do not, since we have *in print* the Doctor's own views, which were published at the same time as his early morning phone call from his grandson.

Very importantly, he begins his exposition (which is also found as chap. 10 in *The Christ-Centred Preaching of Martyn Lloyd-Jones*) with Scripture: "First, we must follow a rule that should always be observed in interpreting Scripture—namely that we should interpret Scripture by Scripture."[9] He begins his study by looking at numerous other passages in the Bible that expound the same thing that is clear from a study of Romans 8:16.

How important this is! It reflects, as he reminds us, the Reformation principle of *sola scriptura*.

What defines, for example, that much debated phrase "the baptism with the Holy Spirit"? A puzzling aspect of this matter is that cessationists discuss it in the terms Pentecostals used at the start of that movement in the early twentieth century: an experience of the Holy Spirit postconversion and evidenced by the gift of miraculous language (or tongues). This is unquestionably what Pentecostal teaching believes—although some of the more Reformed end of that spectrum might today replace "evidenced" with "expected."

[9] Martyn Lloyd-Jones, *Romans: The Sons of God: Exposition of Chapter 8:5–17* (Edinburgh: Banner of Truth, 1974), 296.

So they would say, "Expected by the gift of miraculous language." Cessationists debate the issue as if that is *the* definition, so that if that Pentecostal/charismatic definition is wrong, then the kind of experience that we see in the New Testament therefore has ceased.

Consequently, when the Doctor's views became supposedly clear, all pandemonium broke loose. Some of his followers felt that he had himself become a Pentecostal. Others tried hard to deny that he held the views that were attributed to him, and tried to mold him into their own cessationist theology. When his views were published in another series of his sermons, *Joy Unspeakable*, more dispute broke forth, with many of his cessationist followers feeling that his opinions ought to be suppressed. But as John Caiger, the Doctor's chosen successor as chairman of the Westminster Fellowship of ministers and pastors, assured the family, Dr. Lloyd-Jones's views had been expressed with total clarity in his volume on Romans. His friends in Wales, many of whom he had known since the 1940s, fully endorsed his view. They understood well his use of scriptural terms, and that he held his interpretation without in any way endorsing charismatic or Pentecostal doctrine on the spiritual gifts. They shared his profound concern that there is no life in a graveyard and that dead orthodoxy was dangerous.

And it is clear that the Doctor aims to use *biblical terminology* as his sole determinant of what Christians should and should not believe.

As we noted earlier, many great admirers of the Doctor disagreed with him on this issue; they fully acknowledged that he really did say what he said in his sermons and books. Some, such as Roberts, are among those leading evangelicals in all denominations back to an appreciation of the Doctor and his ministry, a very welcome move. But they feel that he ought to have been more careful in his terminology, as his wording is open to misunderstanding. While that is a fair thing to say, it also misses the point—the Doctor insisted on using *biblical* terminology. If others misused the Bible's expressions, that was no fault of his!

So what, in fact, did Dr. Martyn Lloyd-Jones say about baptism of the Holy Spirit? In describing Romans 8:16, he wrote:

> I suggest that this is a part of "the baptism with the Holy Ghost," or if you prefer it, "the baptism of the Holy Spirit." That is why I referred to John 7:37 to 39 and Acts 2 and so on. Indeed I go further and say that what Paul is describing is the most essential aspect of "the baptism of the Holy Ghost." We said, when dealing with verse 15, that "the Spirit of adoption" is a part of the baptism with the Holy Ghost, but that, as I have just been indicating, is really a preliminary part of that baptism. We cannot be baptized with the Holy Ghost without having the Spirit of adoption, but we can have the Spirit of adoption without knowing this further experience. That is why I say that the most vital and essential part, the essence, of being baptized with the Holy Ghost is that we have this particular form of assurance of our sonship of God. I do not hesitate to say also that this is the same as the "sealing of the Spirit."[10]

Notice how the Doctor quotes from 2 Corinthians 1 and Ephesians 1 and 4. But notice what he goes on to say later in the same sermon:

> Not only so; this experience may be accompanied by various gifts. It was so on the Day of Pentecost. I say "may be," however, for there are variations in this respect, and there is not an exact repetition each time. It is for this reason that those who say that if we have not spoken in tongues we have never been baptized with the Spirit are utterly unscriptural. The Apostle asks in 1 Corinthians 12: "Do all speak with tongues?" The answer is obviously no.[11]

The "earnest" of the Spirit, "sealing with the Spirit," "baptism with the Spirit," are all *biblical* terms that the Doctor, in his clear exposition, regards as interchangeable. We notice two things:

---

[10] Ibid., 300.
[11] Ibid., 305.

1. The baptism or sealing of the Holy Spirit takes place *after* conversion.

2. The Bible itself does not link baptism with any particular gift, including that of "speaking in tongues."

What could be clearer than this? It is obvious that the Doctor regards the baptism with the Spirit as a postconversion experience, one provided by God, and which can, as evidenced in Romans, be a divine means of reinforcing our assurance of salvation as Christians. There is no evidence in anything that he preached at Westminster Chapel and subsequently wrote that suggests that there are two tiers of Christian: those baptized in this way and those not. Neither does he link the experience in any way with a particular gift, whether expected or otherwise.

It is good news that such able and careful expositors as Vaughan Roberts have rediscovered him and his importance and relevance for the twenty-first century. This is especially the case as Roberts and the other new enthusiasts, like J. I. Packer before them, are evangelicals who have remained within historic groupings, such as the Church of England. It is also wonderful that they do *not* seek to straightjacket the Doctor, and are open on where they disagree on *some* issues while lauding him on the *major* ones that unite all true evangelicals.

But when it comes to *this* particular issue, what do we see?

1. Lloyd-Jones uses *biblical*, not man-made, terminology.
2. He is not a cessationist.
3. He is not a Pentecostal.

Dr. Lloyd-Jones was a man who expounded what he felt to be clear and plain from Scripture. That was his prime motive and interest in all he preached and wrote.

Not only that, but as he says in his Romans exposition:

Those passages [from Acts and Revelation] help us understand Romans 8:16, and there are others. Is it not clear to anyone who reads the New Testament without prejudice that the early

Christians, speaking generally, had a spiritual experience and insight and understanding which distinguishes them in a very striking manner from the vast majority of Christians at the present time?[12]

This issue, as many of his followers in Wales understood very well, was one that vexed him greatly, especially in the later years of his life. Why do we no longer have what the early Christians would regard as normal? Or for that matter, that same level of experience that we see in historical revivals down through the centuries?

One can of course disagree with his conclusions and exegesis, including his interpretation of the Epistle to the Romans. In such cases, dissenting is the right thing to do.

But alas, many try to rescue Lloyd-Jones from what they believe to be charismatic corruption by association. They do so with noble motive but without really understanding what he *actually* said. No one was more enthusiastic for the great catechisms of the Reformed period than Martyn Lloyd-Jones. But he saw such statements as reinforcements of the Bible rather than lenses through which we read it.

With the Doctor's own words and Scripture-based methodology so crystal clear, he does not need defenders to explain him away. Today we all too often determine theology through our man-made filters, and think in terms of who today says what, rather than consider Scripture *in practice as well as in theory* as the sole determinant in all matters spiritual and doctrinal. So much too of the discussion has been *ad hominem*: X thinks this, and Y thinks that, and as for Z he *must* be dangerous because he went to a conference with Q in 1963. But if one has a Christ-centered, Scripture-based approach—the two key factors in the Doctor's preaching—none of that matters. It is the teaching of the Bible—*sola scriptura*—rather than the temporary loyalties and affiliations of present-day individuals that determine what we should and should not believe.

Thankfully today—and this is purely my opinion, since speaking

---

[12] Ibid. 298.

for what the Doctor *might have thought* of events more than three decades after his passing is surely ludicrous—new organizations in both the United States and Great Britain focus on a genuine Scripture-based understanding of what the Bible teaches. Nothing man-made can ever be perfect. But such groups include those who differ on the doctrine of baptism and who disagree utterly on the "baptism with the Holy Spirit." It is early days for all this, and we do not know what will happen in the long term. But it is at least encouraging that groups of evangelicals exist with the same total loyalty to Scripture that was such a hallmark of the life and ministry of Martyn Lloyd-Jones.

5

Save Jesus Christ
and Him Crucified

THE DOCTOR AND PREACHING

On Dr. Martyn Lloyd-Jones's gravestone in Wales are the words the apostle Paul wrote to the Corinthians: "For I determined not to know any thing among you, save Jesus Christ, and Him crucified" (1 Cor. 2:2).

It is a fitting epitaph for someone who spent most of his adult life preaching the good news of Jesus Christ crucified and risen, the Savior and Redeemer whose death and resurrection redeems us from our sins and reconciles us to God in salvation.

In some ways, this message is obvious. Of course we as evangelicals believe that this is the only right way to preach.

Or is it that simple?

We know that the reality is more complex. And it is precisely because we have increasingly strayed from the straightforward Pauline/biblical path that we need to heed the words and message of Martyn Lloyd-Jones. For him the nineteenth century was not a time of progress—though materially and scientifically it was certainly that—but an age of disaster. He felt that during that time, evangelicals lost the way and began to preach in ways foreign to Scripture. They had forgotten the Reformation down to the heroic age of Whitefield, Edwards, and the Wesleys in the eighteenth century.

In particular, the Doctor was wary of the innovations introduced by Charles Finney, with the emphasis on making "decisions"—a theology that goes against what the Bible teaches on the role of the Holy Spirit in conversion.

Because of this wariness, the Doctor did not participate in the Billy Graham crusades in Britain, the most famous of which was in 1954, in north London. Graham and Lloyd-Jones met privately, but the entire methodology upon which Graham based his crusades was alien to the Doctor's view of church-based evangelistic preaching. Apart from the emphasis on "decisions," Dr. Lloyd-Jones was also wary of Graham's use of prominent churchmen on the platform. Graham's intention was to give a kind of respectability to his meetings. However, the theology of some of these men was utterly different from the strongly evangelical views that both Graham and the Doctor shared.

It should be noted that it was the *method* and its reliance on human means that Dr. Lloyd-Jones disagreed with. Certainly at that time, Billy Graham was crystal clear in his adherence to the gospel message and, both then as now, abundantly honest in the integrity of his ministry.

Charles Finney is rightly esteemed as an abolitionist; today he is revered by Christians and atheists alike for his zealous campaigning against the evils of slavery. But his theology of the "anxious seat" in which non-Christians were supposed to listen to the proclamation of the gospel is the ancestor of the decision-mentality of many evangelicals ever since. As Dr. Lloyd-Jones reminds us in *Preaching and Preachers*, not even as keen an Arminian as Wesley employed the methodology so familiar to us since Finney.

Today the issue is perhaps more nuanced than it was in the 1970s when the Doctor gave his lectures to the eager students at

Westminster Theological Seminary. We now have seeker-friendly churches, the homogeneous unit principle, and plenty of similar methodologies all well within the evangelical family.

And those of us in the Reformed wing of evangelicalism should never forget the sincerity and evangelistic zeal to save the lost that many Arminian churches possess. The joke that we are the "frozen chosen" is in some ways not so funny, since our tendency toward nonevangelism is quite capable of being worse than many of the groups whose theology we criticize. At least they are engaged in evangelism! They do care profoundly about the spiritually lost, and for those who are evangelical, their motivation is surely biblical in its base.

For the Doctor, preaching was preeminent. We see this in the chapter "No Substitute" (reproduced in our companion volume *The Christ-Centered Preaching of Martyn Lloyd-Jones* in which he makes plain from Scripture and from the long two-thousand-year history of the church that there is no substitute for the preaching of the gospel). Indeed, preaching is the primary task of the church itself and of the preacher—the "pastor-teacher" to use the Pauline terminology, called by God to fulfill this task.

It's true that the Doctor had unique unction in preaching. Not many people can hold an audience for seventy-five minutes, as he could in his later years at Westminster Chapel. In fact his average length was probably just under an hour. But he would say that to preach a faithful, Bible-centered, gospel-based sermon does not mean that *everyone* has to preach for at least sixty minutes! It is quality and faithfulness that count, not length of time.

Recall that the Doctor scrapped many parts of a church service that today many regard as essential to a Sunday service. He realized, for instance, that only inwardly changed lives, people born-again and new in Christ, could escape the curse of alcoholism in South Wales. He therefore jettisoned the temperance work of Sandfields, and saw a large reduction in the amount of heavy drinking and alcoholism. People were converted and wanted to give up alcohol, with the help of the Holy Spirit in their lives. As another evangelical, Alistair Burt, once put it on British television, the "only good spirit is the Holy Spirit." Amen! While temperance was important, it was hearing the gospel that would compel people to turn away from alcoholism.

MUSIC AT THE CHAPEL

No one loved music more than the Doctor; it was one of his main forms of relaxation, especially after a busy Sunday of preaching. Opera and other forms of choral music he appreciated tremendously. So getting rid of the choir at Westminster Chapel when he arrived there in 1938 was not a reflection of his personal views of music, but of his views of the primacy of the biblical method of communicating God's truth, the sermon.

Again, we should not adopt a rigid attitude and say that because he abolished the choir that we should as well. Evangelicals disagree among themselves on the place of music at church. Those of a more contemplative temperament and frame of mind find that music can actually help with the understanding of Scripture; any look at the Old Testament shows that all kinds of musical expression were central to the Jewish people's worship of God.

Huge and often tense discussions can take place in churches between those who like their music soft and others for whom nothing less than full volume suffices. These differences aren't necessarily generational—taste in music can be as much a matter of personality as age. Some churches compromise by having different kinds of music at particular services, others by blending styles at the same service. It is hard to see a biblical mandate for one volume or style of music over another. Nowhere does the Bible prescribe organs or bass guitars!

However, I think that the Doctor would say that these disagreements miss the point, and that our style of music is secondary to the central issue: the exposition of God's Word through a sermon.

We should keep in mind that in Wales, with its world-famous

male voice choirs, choral singing was often a source of secular pride and selfish ambition, as one group sought to outdo its rivals. Many in Wales sang like angels, but their spiritual understanding of the hymns that they so often sang—in award-winning competitions—was wholly negligible. One could and sadly still can hear great hymns sung by drunken men who have no concept of the God about whom they are singing. All too often, in the context in which the Doctor heard such performances, worldliness, not godliness, was at the heart of such music; these songs were not paeans of praise to the Lord but sources of carnal pride.

Dr. Lloyd-Jones also talked of the tyranny of the organist. Today we might refer to the "worship leader" or "minister of music." For the Doctor, the person who chose the music had to be the same person who was preaching the sermon. He thought that the music employed in the service should be preparatory for the Bible passage that was to be expounded.

Many positions in today's churches are not found in the Bible. Some argue that this means that no musical office exists, although the Psalms might well indicate otherwise. But while, for example, we find no reference to a "church manager" in the New Testament, we certainly do find the "gift of administration," which is surely the prerequisite for any managerial post in our churches today. The job of the preacher is *to preach* and to be a pastor to the congregation; that task will be a lot easier if the church has the financial resources to pay someone to do the management and so to free the pastor to do his work

Music, one could therefore argue, is wholly legitimate. But what is its purpose? It is the Holy Spirit working in the hearts of believers, through the exposition of the Bible, that is supposed to warm our hearts and nourish our souls, as the Doctor made clear. Mood music is a human creation, and that is why the *style* of music is irrelevant, whether the hymns of Charles Wesley or the contemporary music of our own time. It is the *purpose* of the music rather than the volume that is the biblical issue at stake.

The congregational singing of Westminster Chapel was extraordinary: over two thousand voices simultaneously proclaiming, participants rather than listeners. There was, perhaps, in such an environment, no need for a choir. This is what the Doctor believed. He wanted the singing of praise to God to be participatory and not a spectacle, with *everyone* singing. He rejected times when those in the congregation observed others praising God on their behalf.

No matter what we think about Lloyd-Jones's position on this, what is clearly biblical is that music should be edifying and text-driven. The hymn and song texts should be informed by Scripture and supported by music in such a way as to bring out the meaning of the text. In other words, music properly used to support a strong text can be another form of biblical exposition or comment. Joint proclamation of scriptural truths is a powerful means of edification. The hymns chosen by the Doctor often fulfilled these criteria.

Today we find many faithful evangelical, gospel-preaching, Christ-centered, Reformed churches with expository sermons that *do* have choirs or people using modern instruments in leading the singing. For the more contemplative (or perhaps introverted) worshipers, *listening* to music can be a profoundly spiritually edifying experience. Such people often find that listening can help them prepare for the sermon to come, and so there is no clash between the words sung by a choir and the exposition from Scripture that then follows.

For some churches, contemporary music is part of the Sunday school. This is true of *Grace Life*, the well-known class of Philip R. Johnson, executive director of Grace to You and based each Sunday at Grace Community Church. Few Sunday school venues are more Reformed and theologically conservative in their doctrine and exposition, yet modern music blends in well in such an atmosphere.

During the Doctor's tenure at the Chapel, All Souls Church, Langham Place, the great evangelical Anglican preaching center, had, under John Stott as rector, both expository ministry and one of the finest Christian orchestras in existence on either side of the

Atlantic. Stott's sermons were wholly expository, and like those of his contemporary a few miles away at the Chapel, many of them are available in print. Today All Souls's musical style is quite diverse, with some services more contemporary, and others retaining a more traditional orchestral sound. Nonetheless, the existence of two churches, both famed for their faithful exposition and Bible-centered approach, but with two very different views on Christian music and worship, shows that there is no one particular pattern that is mandatory if you are to be truly biblical, Christ-centered, and expository. Sermons properly delivered are perhaps compatible with either approach.

So it is the principle that counts. If one agrees with the Doctor that the exposition of God's Word Sunday after Sunday is utmost, then we can work out for ourselves how to apply that principle in the way best suited to where God has put us.

Music is also misused as a means of getting people to attend services. It is of course far better to have quality music than a dirge, which does no glory to God and more harm than good. But as the Doctor's lifelong refrain reminds us, it is the unction and spiritual quality of the preaching that is at the heart of what makes a church truly alive.

It is also true to say that if we have a Reformed understanding of how people come to salvation, we can employ the music we want, and feel it is theologically and musically appropriate for our congregation, rather than feel obliged to have a particular style out of fear that if we do not, then people will not attend. The issue of what kind of music to employ should be one discussed for its own sake rather than out of terror of being seen as old-fashioned. If the preaching has true unction, then the people will come—and it will be God who brings them.

In *Preaching and Preachers* the Doctor reiterates the futility of the endless fads and fashions that people use to try to get people into church. As he showed, sometimes clergy who were popular in the secular sphere (such as commentators on nuclear weapons or social justice) also had churches that were virtually empty on Sundays. They had fame but not unction! And of course one could add that numbers alone mean nothing—some of the most notorious "prosperity" teachers have packed congregations with people longing for their own gold Cadillac. Others of similarly dubious theology bring in thousands in the same way that one could expect of a famous circus. But many churches struggle. They are forever looking for some infallible formula that will take them from empty to maximum capacity overnight.

As Dr. Lloyd-Jones reflected, all such attempts will fail. But what is interesting is that as evangelicals we so often fall for them, especially those that are well-intentioned. Or we overcriticize them, forgetting that the sincerity of those trying to use such methods is genuine; they often wish to seek and to save the lost. Either way we end up being credulous or uncharitable, neither of which is a good position to take.

Here one cannot forget the Doctor's worldview, his overarching systematic theology and approach. Believing in the doctrines of grace, the Bible's account of how it is the Holy Spirit who convicts people of their sin and need of repentance, really does make a practical as well as theological difference. It is *God* who saves, not human endeavor, and so by definition, human-centered attempts cannot be the magic bullet for which we often long. God can use all sorts of means through which to save people, and in his infinite love and mercy he will enable sinners to be born again through all variety of methodologies, which is something many of us can easily forget. But that does not excuse us for using our own methods rather than God's.

Dr. Lloyd-Jones was what we would now call counterintuitive. Rather than wanting people to feel comfortable in church, he wanted the message of salvation to make them profoundly *uncomfortable*. We are sinners without a single solitary hope of saving ourselves, and few things can be as unsettling as that. People hearing the good news should feel convicted rather than relaxed!

So how has this change in evangelical thinking, one that so concerned the Doctor, persisted? When did we become pragmatists? It is surely that we are Reformed in name and Arminian in practice, as in so many parts of life. (For example, Dr. Lloyd-Jones was utterly aghast at parents trying to pressure their children into professing conversion—a natural and spiritual wish based in love, but not at all in step with the teaching of Scripture on salvation.) Do we truly believe in the convicting, redeeming, and sovereign power of the Holy Spirit, or do we not?

While the unction of a Martyn Lloyd-Jones comes seldom in a generation, God is at work in churches faithful to his Word. If, like the Doctor, we adopt the *principles* of Scripture, then we know we can trust the Holy Spirit to do his work in those who are lost.

Today we often forget that in *their* times, Isaac Watts, John Newton, and Charles Wesley were all new and contemporary, so there is no particular merit in singing hymns over a century old. But we also do not need to be afraid to sing only those songs composed within the last decade. We have a choice, and divisions over church music can distract us from whether the Bible is expounded properly in both music and sermon. The Doctor loved quoting from the words of the great eighteenth-century hymns, and it is surely the lyrics themselves that are important rather than when the song was composed or the volume at which it is played. There is also no point, surely, in being musically loyal for its own sake to whatever kind of song (eighteenth-century vs. contemporary) one espouses if the centrality of the sermon and its exposition is forgotten. And how about variety: whether fourth-century, eighteenth-century, or contemporary? Surely so long as the words of the songs or hymns tie in with what is about to be preached, the century in which it was written should not matter. Understanding and embracing the sung text in our lives does.

We do not have to agree with what the Doctor did at Westminster Chapel, therefore, to agree with his *principles*, which were Bible-based and Christ-centered.

In addition, we should not forget the practical implications of the sovereignty of God, especially in matters of evangelism. It is the Holy Spirit who convicts, not our efforts. As J. I. Packer points out so successfully, it is our job to be faithful and that of the Holy Spirit to convert. It is the faithful witness of Christian believers throughout the week and over the years that often speaks most to non-Christians. Our lifestyle can speak volumes. Here one can agree with what many of the Billy Graham team tell us, that conversions happen because of years of previous friendship between a Christian and their hitherto unbelieving friends. We see this in the book of Acts, and in the history of the church through the centuries.

Above all, perhaps, both the Doctor and Packer are right to say that those who understand the message of Scripture, the truth of the work of the Holy Spirit, and the nature of the doctrines of grace can be more confident than those for whom human effort is everything. We can have confidence because of who God is (which is why Calvin put his exposition of grace in his section on the nature of God rather than in a section on evangelism).

The Doctor eschewed drama and other similar human methodologies. Need we do the same? It is surely a mistake to be legalistic, but equally it is an error to be human-centered in our approach. Is the drama a mere distraction? Or does it prepare viewers for the Bible exposition that follows?

THE DOCTOR AND APOLOGETICS

Dr. Lloyd-Jones was also uncertain about the need for apologetics. He always cut straight to the chase! His contemporary Francis Schaeffer took another view, as does Tim Keller today. But the Doctor also realized that conversion could be a slow process. He knew from Scripture that someone whom God predestined could never die before the moment of conversion (the perennial Arminian's nightmare), and that time taken to a genuine conversion was always better than a human-inspired rush that turns out to be false. Here we can see the influence of his medical training. He knew from his extensive study of psychology that people can be persuaded to make emotional decisions that in the long-term have no meaning. (The kind of "decision time" music often played at some events particularly troubled him.) He illustrates this at length in *Preaching and Preachers*, and it makes salutary reading for all of us today.

Schaeffer, however, a man as thoroughly Bible-based and Christ-centered and theologically Reformed as the Doctor, felt that one of the issues Christians face is that non-Christians simply have no background knowledge or understanding of any kind of biblical truth whatsoever. As Os Guinness (a former member of the Westminster Chapel congregation and profound admirer of the Doctor) has also said, Schaeffer in many ways predicted postmodernism long before the term was invented. We live in an era in which people do not so much have a wrong idea of God, but reject his very existence altogether. And as for the concept of sin, the very nature of it presupposes a belief in absolutes, in the existence of right and wrong, that simply no longer exists.

Apologetics, in this view, is not a substitute for preaching the cross and the need for repentance, but a vital introduction to people whose mind-sets are now profoundly and utterly separate from the ways of God. We are in many ways back in the days of Paul's epistle to the Romans, in terms of degeneracy and contempt for morality. The difference is that our state is now linked to atheism rather than to the worship of Jupiter or Mars. Paul's sermon to the Athenians is surely a form of apologetics, since he uses their background and belief system to point them in the one and only true direction of Jesus Christ.

Theologically conservative, Bible-centered, Reformed believers—such as Schaeffer and Keller—want to show people the futility of the postmodern worldview. And having done that, they then open to them the truth in Scripture of salvation through the cross. As Schaeffer put it, we have to start where the Bible does: "In the beginning God . . ."

But of course people still have to know they are sinners, as the

Doctor's numerous published evangelistic sermons remind us. In one of his famous sermons (now published in *The Cross*), he used John F. Kennedy's death to show that only the risen Jesus, rather than the dead Kennedy, was the answer; the Doctor was very aware of the way in which events would regularly show the need for people to turn to Christ for salvation.

Perhaps therefore, *in practice*, there is only a scintilla of difference between the two approaches. When Paul was in Athens, he addressed the crowd in Greek, not in Aramaic. But while the *language* he used was that of his hearers, the *message* was the same. The Doctor addressed his own London congregation not in Welsh or in seventeenth-century English but in the contemporary English of his own day. People need to know that they must be reconciled to God and that we are all fallen and hopeless sinners, but in the sad times in which we live they need to realize that God exists and that sin is an absolute unchanging truth that has not disappeared with horse carriages and gas lamps. What the Bible says is as true in the twenty-first century as it was in the first.

In the Doctor's day it was common to bring non-Christian friends to church. Now the practice is often similar to that of the early church, when Christians shared the gospel in the marketplace, or, as Paul did at Athens, in a place where non-Christians gathered to discuss ideas. The concept of having evangelistic Bible studies in secular cafes is a twenty-first-century update of a first-century practice, with a coffee shop taking the place of a street market or of Mars Hill. Many people subsequently converted at church have been prepared for the gospel message by what they have heard at a local Starbucks from their Christian friends. In fact one could say that many of our contemporary practices are more biblical than some like to admit.

THE DOCTOR AGAINST MAN-MADE CONTRIVANCES

But despite the naysayers and the doubters of the power of the Holy Spirit, despite the despondent Arminianism so dominant even in churches that claim to be Reformed, many are converted, as they have been for millennia, by sermons heard in church.

One of the strongest justifications for the kind of ministry that existed at the Chapel in the Doctor's time is that he had a literally global congregation. Countless nationalities were present each week, and people from the working class to friends of royalty sat side by side every Sunday. The spectrum of people invited to hear Dr. Lloyd-Jones preach his evangelistic sermons in the evening was considerable. His was no "homogeneous unit principle" congregation, of congregants of similar lifestyle or economic or educational background. Few churches would have professors and building laborers sitting next to each other, listening to the same sermon.

Perhaps this is easier in a cosmopolitan area such as London, which in those days was still an imperial capital city of an empire upon which the sun famously never set. The fact that working class people who left school as teenagers listened alongside medical students was a unique symbol of the unifying power of the Holy Spirit and of the Word of God. The Doctor despised reliance on Madison Avenue or the latest sociological theories; the congregation who heard him preach was living proof that no man-made technique is necessary to bring people in.

The Doctor also strongly eschewed the politicization of the message of the cross. No one could ever tell the politics of those who attended the Chapel, and if one had conducted a poll, one would find a large cross section of all the political standpoints of the time, from left to right.

How many different political persuasions do you have in your church? In Britain there is no evangelical default position politically speaking, since all "matters of conscience" are decided by members of Parliament as individuals rather than as representatives of a political party. There are pro-choice Conservatives and pro-life Labour, and on the recent issue of gay marriage the voting went across political lines, with evangelicals and Catholics of different parties voting usually one way and those in favor of change voting the other. In Britain, saying that one is a "committed Christian" does not reveal how one might vote.

In the Doctor's day the Free Churches that were political were usually on the liberal/left. Social issues had huge importance, and many preachers were both politically and theologically liberal, with large numbers involved, for example, in the Campaign for Nuclear Disarmament. Then there were those, often influenced by the United States, who were deeply worried about Communism. The Doctor's ministry after 1945 was entirely in the context of the Cold War, since that conflict did not end until eight years after his death.

So in the British context, many a pulpit had sermons against social injustice, or against the horrors of nuclear war, or against the perils of Communism, and of the atheistic USSR taking over the world.

In Britain today many churches of a theologically liberal persuasion still have an interest and involvement in social issues. Some evangelical churches do as well, it should be said, but are careful not to compromise the preaching of the gospel. The Doctor's son-in-law, Sir Frederick Catherwood, was active in social programs while president of the Evangelical Alliance, helping, as he would put it, by giving soup to the unemployed as well as the message of Jesus Christ from the pulpit. Other British evangelical churches are wary of social action, given its close links in the past to liberal theology. Dr. Lloyd-Jones was probably more in the latter category, but he did enthusiastically support members of his congregation who were involved in welfare activities in poorer parts of London. His encouragement of Elizabeth Braund, who ran a youth center called Providence House in one of the capital's roughest areas, is an example.

But so far as preaching politics from the pulpit, he could not be more against it, and never hesitated to denounce those who did so. To him politicians of any kind were no substitute for the urgent need of salvation in Jesus Christ. Only the new birth that happens at conversion can change anyone, spiritually and from the inside.

As he put it so firmly in *Life in the Spirit*:

The deduction we therefore draw is that the church's task primarily is to evangelize, and to bring people to a knowledge of God. Then, having done that, she is to teach them how to live their life under God as His people. The church is not here to reform the world, for the world cannot be reformed. The business of the church is to evangelize, to preach the Gospel of salvation to men who are blinded by sin and under the domination and the power of the devil. The moment the church begins to enter into the details of politics and economics, she is doing something that militates against her primary task of evangelism.[1]

He went on to say something that surely will resonate with evangelicals for whom politically partisan preaching from the pulpit has become the norm:

As one obvious example, take the case of the church and communism. My contention is that it is not the business of the Christian church to be denouncing communism. . . . It is wrong for this reason, that the primary task of the church is to evangelize communists, to open their eyes, to bring them to conviction and to conversion.[2]

He goes on to say what should be obvious, but which is in danger of being forgotten in many faithful, gospel-preaching evangelical churches today:

Whatever the position or political views of men, whether they are communists or capitalists or anything else, we are to regard them all as sinners, and equally sinners. They are all lost, they are all damned, they all need to be converted, they all need to be born again.[3]

Like Spurgeon, the Doctor was a firm Calvinist. But also like Spurgeon, he knew that one should not have human hindrances to

---

[1] Lloyd-Jones, *Life in the Spirit in Marriage, Home and Work: An Exposition of Ephesians 5:18 to 6:9* (Edinburgh: Banner of Truth, 1973), 318–19.
[2] Ibid., 319.
[3] Ibid.

the preaching of salvation—the very nature of the Christian message, of everyone being a sinner in need of being saved, is offensive enough without adding any man-made obstacles!

As he put it:

> So the church looks on the world and its peoples in an entirely different way from non-Christians. If the church therefore spends her time in denouncing communism she is more or less shutting the door of evangelism among communists as firmly as possible. The communist says, "Your Christianity is just anti-communist and pro-capitalist; I am not going to listen to the message." Therefore you cannot evangelise him. The church is not meant to deal with political and other positions directly, her task is to preach her Gospel to all and sundry whatever they are, and to bring them to a knowledge of Christ.[4]

It is important to keep to the principle of not reading Dr. Lloyd-Jones's views in the past into conditions in the present, more than three decades after his death.

Nonetheless, we can still learn from the Doctors' approach to the pulpit today.

Many evangelicals are careful to preach the gospel in the way that Dr. Lloyd-Jones prescribed. One would not know their politics from their sermons. People of all political persuasions and none attend their churches, and non-Christians are converted and find spiritual new life in Jesus Christ.

This is surely true of many fine churches in the United States. Capitol Hill Baptist Church in Washington, DC, is one such congregation. There are Republicans and Democrats in the congregation, many of whom have deeply held political convictions. But as evangelical Christians, they unite every Sunday with thanks to God for the far more important thing that they all share in common, their faith in Jesus Christ as their personal Savior and Lord. And the fact that people from both sides of the Hill, not to mention the strong

---

[4] Ibid.

racial mix, are present in the congregation speaks volumes for the transforming power of the gospel. The Reformed, thoroughly evangelical, expository ministry found there Sunday after Sunday makes it a church very much in the mold of Martyn Lloyd-Jones.

But I can think of the minister of another church, equally evangelical and gospel-focused, who, near election time, personally endorsed the tea party nominee for the Republican nomination to state office and who used the public platform within the church to proclaim *as Christian truth* the political message of that group. Imagine the effect this had on Democratic visitors to that church! They did not hear the gospel—which was faithfully proclaimed in a careful expository way—but rather the tea party message that was proclaimed from the same platform. It was a recent example of the same principle that the Doctor expressed in *Life in the Spirit*—that if one equates the gospel with a political viewpoint, people of that view, whether Communist in the 1960s or Democrat today, simply will not hear a word said about the message of Jesus Christ.

The Doctor had no problem with individual members of his congregation, or indeed any evangelical Christian, having strong political beliefs. *But the pulpit was no place for politics.* The church should not be politically aligned.

Everyone needs the gospel. So we come again to the words on the Doctor's tombstone, from the apostle Paul: "For I determined not to know any thing among you, save Jesus Christ, and him crucified." That is *the* message for all time, for all people, and for all places. It never changes. Neither should we.

6

Accentuating
the Positive

MARTYN LLOYD-JONES THE
GLOBAL CHRISTIAN

Bing Crosby once crooned, "Accentuate the positive." That ditty will be the guiding feature of this chapter, which examines the vexing issue of Martyn Lloyd-Jones and his doctrine of evangelical unity.

The speech Martyn Lloyd-Jones made at a meeting of the Evangelical Alliance in October 1966 proved to be one of his most controversial utterances. He argued, in effect, that evangelicals should not be separated from each other in different denominations, but should come together in evangelical unity, and should do so for the sake of the gospel. Because this was a prophetic call rather than a detailed action plan, his summons for evangelicals to forget denominational loyalties in favor of a larger evangelical affiliation has been widely misunderstood.

One of the most tragic ways in which the Doctor is misunderstood involves his views on the nature of the church, on how evangelicals ought to associate with one another, and on what arrangements they should make as a result. In particular, the last fifteen years of his fifty-four in ministry (1966–1981) have been interpreted in a wholly negative light, with some defining the Doctor by what he was *against* rather than what he was *for*.

Thankfully, objective books are now being written that put Dr. Lloyd-Jones into his proper historical context, by people without an axe to grind either way.

My aim is to reinterpret the issue in a way that is historical, irenic, and positive, and especially to look at Lloyd-Jones and his definition of evangelical unity in a way that recent studies, either polemical or academic, have not.

So we need to ask:

1. What was the dispute in October 1966 that caused all the fuss?
2. How has it been interpreted and misrepresented?
3. What was his role in the International Fellowship of Evangelical Students and in global worldwide evangelical unity?

The third question will get us to the heart of what he actually believed and stood for as an evangelical Christian. One of the major defects of much of the study on Martyn Lloyd-Jones, even the thoughtful and academic research now appearing, is that it completely omits the global aspect of Dr. Lloyd-Jones. It is fascinating to look at him as a Welshman, for instance (see *Engaging with Martyn Lloyd-Jones*). But the "whole problem," to use one of his favorite phrases, is that books tend, perhaps understandably, to be very British-centered. His major ministry was of course at Westminster Chapel from 1938–1968, and he lived for most of each year in the United Kingdom, especially as he ceased to be able to travel so much. But he spent much of the year, when in better health, in the United States. And his link with the International Fellowship of Evangelical Students lasted from the late 1930s until his death in 1981.

IFES was by definition an entirely *evangelical* organization. It was also global, with member movements literally all over the world. Today in 2014 it remains evangelical, having a basis of faith in which Lloyd-Jones played a major drafting role.

His time with IFES was wholly positive and thoroughly evangelical, with none of the negative connotations that his denigrators wish to bestow upon him. In chapter 4 we noted his three talks to the IFES titled "What Is an Evangelical?" Those talks define how he perceived the term *evangelical*. However, as we all know, times change, and in 2015 we can see that however controversial he might have been at the time, he was also being prophetic. Those were three talks, but it was a single address in 1966 that caused controversy.

I must note that not all of the Doctor's own family agreed with him in his lifetime (although some did then and zealously do so now). His brother-in-law and oldest friend was Ieuan Phillips. When Phillips died, the Doctor told his wife (Ieuan's sister) that he had lost his best friend. Yet when Phillips was asked not just to stay in the Welsh Presbyterian Church (known to most as the Welsh Calvinistic Methodists), but to become their moderator, he did so. The two brothers-in-law did not agree, but that never altered their deep and close friendship that spanned decades.

Martyn Lloyd-Jones never broke friendship with theologian Philip Edgcumbe Hughes, of Westminster Theological Seminary and an ordained Anglican minister. The same was true of his friendship with John Gwyn Thomas, a Welshman as well as an Anglican vicar. Ironically, Thomas was the successor at St. Paul's in Cambridge to Herbert Carson, one of the select number of leading evangelical Anglicans to secede in response to the Doctor's call.

Lloyd-Jones was also very close to his brother, Sir Vincent Lloyd-Jones. Sir Vincent was High Church, or Anglo-Catholic. But the two brothers were devoted friends, loved making everyone laugh, and discussed deep matters of faith. While Sir Vincent remained Anglo-Catholic to the end, the Doctor's family strongly believe that the two brothers had reached a good understanding of each other.

So now we come to the substantive issue.

THE CONTROVERSY OF 1966

What was the issue back in 1966, and how has a speech become so seriously misunderstood, and with such dire results? Let us examine this as objectively as possible.

Evangelicals in the Church of England had been discussing their relationship to the denomination. At the same time, liberals in the Baptist Union had been making controversial statements, one of which denied the divinity of Christ. So some evangelical Baptists were worried about being in the same body as those who attacked the gospel. And evangelical Anglicans worried that they were seen by fellow Anglicans as people who had split loyalties—to other Anglicans within the denomination and to evangelicals outside it. It is important to remember that all this was going on before the Doctor spoke, and that this was the context of his speech. The Evangelical Alliance asked him to speak, having full knowledge of his views. What he said that night in London, to a packed audience, was thus no surprise.

One of the great problems that arose in the controversy that followed his speech is that not everyone was clear on precisely what he said and did not say. Thankfully, it is now published in full, in *Knowing the Times*.

In the light of subsequent debate and, alas, ill will, it is astonishing, rereading the speech nearly half a century later, how irenic it is. (While I was present in the balcony, relying on the memory of an eleven-year-old boy is not a good idea! Unfortunately, many people do rely solely on their own memories.)

Lloyd-Jones's talk was never intended to be an appeal for evangelicals to *leave*. It was aimed at *all* evangelicals, certainly not just those in the Church of England, something his Free Church defenders and Anglican critics often overlook.

And Iain Murray is right—Martyn Lloyd-Jones was not an organization man. He was not trying to found an all-evangelical grand denomination. What he wanted was "a fellowship, or an association, of evangelical churches."[1] No superdenomination was ever

---

[1] Martyn Lloyd-Jones, "Evangelical Unity: An Appeal," in *Knowing the Times* (Edinburgh: Banner of Truth, 1989), 257.

planned, and it certainly never crossed his mind. Even those who knew him well, such as J. I. Packer, alas misunderstood him here: his was not a call to create structures but a prophetic appeal for Christian witness.

As Lloyd-Jones put it in his 1967 New Year's letter to his own church, Westminster Chapel (which left the Congregational Union to join the FIEC), what he had in mind was simply:

> An appeal . . . to all truly Evangelical people in all the denominations to come together and to form local independent Evangelical churches which should be a loose fellowship together in order that the world might hear and see a living witness to the truth of the Gospel. . . . We are living in momentous times, undoubtedly one of the great turning-points of history. The opportunity for Evangelical witness is unique, the possibilities are tremendous. Are we equal to the times?[2]

Gordon Murray, editor of the magazine *English Churchman*, was one of many leading evangelical Anglicans who did secede. His insight is significant:

> He [Dr. Lloyd-Jones] was not putting forward some negative scheme into which we are reluctantly forced, but rather was pointing us to the glorious opportunity of taking positive action in the ecumenical sphere, of coming together as Christians, not because other people's errors demand it, but because we want to, and we realise we ought to if we are to be true to our Evangelical convictions.[3]

In other words, the Doctor was arguing for unity, not for division or schism. As he said in his talk to the IFES: "You and I are Evangelicals. We are agreed about these essentials of the faith, and yet we are divided from one another."[4] Evangelicals in theologically

---

[2] Lloyd-Jones to the congregation of Westminster Chapel (London: Westminster Chapel Archives), January 1, 1967, quoted in Andrew Atherstone and David Ceri Jones, eds., *Engaging with Martyn Lloyd-Jones: The Life and Legacy of "The Doctor"* (Nottingham: Apollos, 2011), 273.
[3] Ibid.
[4] Lloyd-Jones, "Evangelical Unity," 254.

mixed denominations were always having to distinguish themselves from those in their own denomination who denied the truth. But outsiders saw only the "visible unity" of a denomination, not the unity on vital issues of faith that evangelicals of different denominations had in common with one another. "Let me therefore," he continued, "make an appeal to you evangelical people here this evening. What reasons have we for not coming together?"[5]

He continued:

> What cogent reason have we for staying as we are when we have this new, and as I regard it, heaven-sent opportunity for doing something new? . . . Let me put it positively. Do we not feel the call to come together, not occasionally, but *always*? It is a grief to me that I spend so little of my time with some of my brethren. I want to spend the whole of my time with them. I am a believer in ecumenicity, evangelical ecumenicity.[6]

The wholly positive nature of his appeal could not be clearer or more abundantly plain!

But alas he was misunderstood almost as soon as his words were uttered! John Stott, anxious that many a keen evangelical curate might secede in the light of the Doctor's oratory, took the unusual step of using his chairman's prerogative to contradict the speaker. This set many a cat among the proverbial pigeons, and led many to believe, wrongly, that the Doctor was "anti-Anglican." In fact it was evident that he was in favor of evangelicals from *all* denominations coming together, and his appeal to evangelicals in other denominations, such as the Baptist Union or the Welsh Presbyterians, was a huge success.

A great storm erupted after the event, mainly from Anglican writers. But they and others misunderstood (then and since, one could argue) that the Doctor was addressing a far wider audience.

Recent research by Andrew Atherstone and others, in *Engaging with Martyn Lloyd-Jones*, has revealed that the Doctor's appeal in

---

[5] Ibid.
[6] Ibid., 255.

1966 was far more successful than many have realized. Many Anglicans did leave the Church of England, maybe not immediately, but in a definite trickle over the years that followed. What is also interesting is that, as Atherstone shows, many evangelicals in that denomination had *already* left by 1966, and for the reasons that the Doctor outlined in his famous address.

However, even Atherstone's chapter on the subject is titled "Lloyd-Jones and the Anglican Secession Crisis." Since it was John Stott's remarks in relation to the Doctor's address that accentuated focus on the Anglicans in the audience, this is entirely understandable. But it is also deeply misleading. For among Free Church people, in denominations such as the Baptist Union or the Congregationalists or the Welsh (Calvinistic Methodist) Presbyterians, the Doctor's appeal had rousing success.

As Atherstone shows, many evangelicals in the Church of England still believed in the concept of a *territorial* church—it is the Church *of England*. Many of the godly folk who stayed within their denomination actually did so for what they strongly believed to be gospel reasons. They were not—in their view—defending a decision to stay inside a theologically compromised denomination, but choosing *as evangelicals* to stay within what they sincerely held to be God's means of proclaiming biblical truth to the English, the country in which God had put them.

Baptists or Congregationalists do not possess such a territorial vision, and Martyn Lloyd-Jones, patriotic Welshman though he was, most certainly rejected anything like it! To him, the whole idea of a "Christian country" was biblical nonsense. The church was and is God's elect people—*Christians*.

As he felt strongly through such international groupings as the IFES, evangelicals across the world have infinitely more in common with each other as brothers and sisters in Christ than they do with non-Christian members of their own race or nation. The church consists of *people*, and the whole idea of a territorial church perplexed him completely. Needless to say, people from the Free

Churches had the same view on this issue as he. And as Don Carson has so rightly pointed out, the Doctor, being Welsh as well as evangelical, would naturally find so English a worldview utterly alien.

However, many in the Church of England—whom Lloyd-Jones recognized as fellow evangelicals in his speech—saw the issue not so much in terms of believing in a territorial church *per se* but in using the existence of a territorial church as a means created by God to enable the evangelism of England. In other words, they wanted to remain where they were not out of some delusion that they could take over the denomination—which was politically impossible in a state-controlled church—but to remain in it as a clear evangelical witness, using the status of the denomination as the official national church as a means of evangelism. This might seem odd to those of us used to a different model of ecclesiology, but it is vital to say that these were evangelicals staying within the church for wholly evangelical reasons.

One of the best of them was Keith Weston, not so widely known today but someone who spent over a quarter of a century as rector of St. Ebbe's in Oxford, one of the few evangelical churches that has for centuries remained loyal to its evangelical roots. Interestingly, St. Ebbe's is where both of the Doctor's daughters, Elizabeth and Ann, attended when they were students at Oxford University, and it is where I attended when I was a student there in the 1970s.

Weston clearly stated the position of Bible-preaching and Bible-believing conservative evangelicals of that time:

> I am innocent enough to believe that the Church of England needs its committed Evangelicals now probably as never before. It would be a terrible tragedy if we were all to leave now. As one respected Evangelical in this City once said, "Only rats leave a sinking ship!" Has not God put us here (with all the resulting problems) precisely because He has a job for us here?[7]

Evangelicals were, Weston continued, to "uphold the Truth of the Gospel for which our Church of England martyrs died." (In Oxford

---

[7] Ibid., 276.

we were always conscious of the Anglican martyrs of Mary I's reign. The place at which they were burned at the stake was just outside my college, and thousands of us would walk across it every day.)

The point that many forget is to put together evangelicals in the Church of England who were in reality staying for different reasons—who are now best described as "open evangelicals" and for whom denominational affiliation and action became a major goal—and the more conservative variety who stayed in for what they believed to be wholly gospel reasons. (And we should not forget that *doctrinally* John Stott was wholly in the second category, as the rest of his life bore witness, from the 1970s onward.)

One thing does need to be mentioned. When Dr. Lloyd-Jones was seriously ill in 1968, Stott visited him in the hospital, and the two men made up fully for their division in 1966. Sadly, biographies of these two men leave this out. But it is very important to remember. And the close friendship of Elizabeth Lloyd-Jones and J. I. Packer, which goes back to their undergraduate days at Oxford, has continued to this day. Fred and Elizabeth Catherwood and Jim and Kit Packer have remained close friends for nearly seventy years.

One regrettable feature of the debate is that many involved freeze everything in time as it was in 1966, ignoring what has happened in the evangelical world since then. Because Lloyd-Jones died in 1981, he could not possibly comment on events that occurred decades later! Many people have tried to reclaim him retrospectively, which is surely impossible. To use a noncontentious issue as an example, many evangelicals in Wales today are supporters of Plaid Cymru, which in English translates to "the Party of Wales." The Doctor's brother Vincent knew the founding father of Plaid Cymru, the late Gwynfor Evans. Evans's admiration for the Doctor was considerable, even though it was based on respect for a distinguished fellow countryman and not on theology. But apart from the fact that the Doctor *never* gave political endorsements and would regard such a request as wholly inappropriate, it is impossible for us today to know what the Doctor would have thought about Plaid Cymru!

The same is true of today's theological and evangelical scene. In a sense, it is utterly ludicrous—to use words he often employed—to speculate on what he would have said about issues of the twenty-first century.

In the immediate aftermath of 1966, one could say that many regrettable things happened. Critics of the Catherwood/McGrath thesis—which stated that the separatists became increasingly hard-line and unkind to those, such as J. I. Packer, who did not agree with the Doctor—expressed their disagreement in various reviews of Alister McGrath's biography of Packer.[8] But the idea that many Free Church people froze out J. I. Packer is, as McGrath argues, sadly all too true. Note that in 1966 the Doctor did not advocate any breaking of fellowship between evangelicals who agreed with him and those who did not. He himself kept contact with many who disagreed with him, his own family included.

At the time it seemed to many of us that much of the ill will and separatism that ensued proved all too well the thinking of the great evangelical thinker and apologist, Francis Schaeffer. He himself had split from a denomination that he felt had gone doctrinally astray. But he also realized two things:

1. That among those who leave, a sense of spiritual superiority can creep in, along with a bitterness to those who have not separated.
2. That among those who stay, an increasing tendency to compromise can emerge, with the dividing line between staying and leaving receding ever further into the distance.

Sadly, one can argue that Schaeffer was vindicated. Soon evangelicals who had separated from their denominations would break fellowship with evangelicals who chose to remain. Many—but significantly not all—evangelical Anglicans became more involved with the structures of the Church of England. And then some Lloyd-Jones followers invented second-degree separation: for example, if someone in an FIEC or Grace Baptist Church, which had separated,

---

[8] Atherstone, "Introduction," in Atherstone and Jones, *Engaging with Martyn Lloyd-Jones*, 20.

had fellowship with evangelical Anglicans, the hard-liners would not have fellowship with *him*, because even though he had separated, he spoke to those who had not!

Such attitudes were far from the infinitely more irenic tone that the Doctor proclaimed in 1966.

Some writers ignore all the changes that have occurred within the evangelical wing of the Church of England, as numerous evangelical Anglicans, led by R. C. Lucas of St. Helen's Bishopsgate and others, engaged in a massive rethink. As Melvin Tinker, Christopher Idle, and David Searle all have pointed out in articles down the years, those who ignore this major development are guilty of "astonishing selectivity." They acknowledge the work of Dick Lucas, the Proclamation Trust, the Evangelical Ministry Assembly, Oak Hill Theological College, and the missionary society Crosslinks. The existence of such groups, these people demonstrate, shows the shift within the major wing of evangelical Anglicanism toward a kind of primary self-identity *as evangelicals* rather than as *Anglicans*. This is, of course, the very thing for which the Doctor had called.

Speakers such as John MacArthur have been warmly welcomed by Dick Lucas to the Evangelical Ministry Assembly in London. The audience of the EMA has been as much (evangelical) Free Church as (evangelical) Anglican. A movement such as Reform, aimed not so much at participating in Anglican structures as bringing back gospel-centered, Bible-based conservative evangelicalism into the Church of England, is yet another example.

Some of the defenders of Dr. Lloyd-Jones might ignore all of these positive recent developments, because, for them the Doctor was a historical icon rather than a living flesh-and-blood human being. Dr. Gaius Davies, a lifelong friend of many of the Lloyd-Jones family, in *Genius, Grief, and Grace* has argued that this is a problem in coming to terms with an objective consideration of the Doctor's life and ministry.[9] (Here it should be said that he was not

---

[9] Gaius Davies, *Genius, Grief, and Grace* (Ross-shire, UK: Christian Focus, 2008). Note that earlier editions do not contain a chapter on the Doctor's life.

only at the wedding of the Doctor's elder daughter, Elizabeth, to Fred Catherwood, but a guest at the Catherwood golden wedding anniversary as well. Here again, differences over Martyn Lloyd-Jones's beliefs did not impede friendships.)

The idea of Martyn Lloyd-Jones as an icon is, needless to say, a profoundly controversial one! My main job is writing about twentieth-century history, and of the career of Sir Winston Churchill in particular. As one of Churchill's strongly evangelical descendants has put it, God is God, and Winston Churchill was not God. But in many circles today, to admit that Churchill ever made so much as a single error is to commit blasphemy of a heinous kind. Because Churchill saved not only Britain in 1940 but arguably Western democracy and civilization itself, does not mean that he was infallible throughout his sixty-four years of public life.

We realize the same is true of Martyn Lloyd-Jones. *And that is how he himself would have wanted to be viewed.* Gaius Davies is surely right to say that to turn a man into an icon is not helpful to the man himself. There have been ludicrous attempts to rewrite what the Doctor actually said and believed about issues such as the doctrine of the Holy Spirit. However, it is a mistake to say that Dr. Lloyd-Jones brooked no criticism, or did not want contradiction. What he found, to his sorrow, was that people were often so in awe of him that they felt unable to speak their minds back. So he would argue with his own descendants in the happy knowledge that he had trained us always to answer back if we disagreed with him! And as with his best friend and brother-in-law, Ieuan Phillips, and others in his family who rejected his view, *as evangelicals* in loving disagreement, the deep love and family solidarity that bound them all continued completely unchanged. (Here I should say that others in the family agreed with the Doctor totally.)

GLOBAL OUTLOOK

Today we can argue that the global situation has shifted in the direction that the Doctor wished in his speech in October 1966—before his words became twisted by both sides. Some have argued that the Doctor could have done something to prevent the misconceptions. But I think that as he grew older—and increasingly frail, down to his death in 1981—what started as a firm position became ever more hard-line and ossified as time progressed.

But now we can accentuate the positive, something that has not always been possible.

The Doctor always put evangelical loyalty above that of, say, a denomination, and even above whether someone, such as a godly evangelical of Arminian views, accepted the doctrines of grace. And today we bear witness to an utter transformation of the *global* Anglican Church or Communion. Dr. Lloyd-Jones was far more aware of events in other countries than many who have, in essence, only looked at him within a British context. There are, for example, seventeen times as many Anglicans attending a church every Sunday in Nigeria than in Britain. And while in the United Kingdom only half of those are professing evangelicals, the considerable majority of them in Nigeria fall into a conservative evangelical theological category. While the majority in southern Africa or the United States are liberal, in West and East Africa, in Spanish-speaking Latin America, and in other parts of the world, millions of Anglicans—archbishops and other leaders included—are overwhelmingly Bible-based conservative evangelicals.

In other words, in terms of the *worldwide* Anglican Communion, as represented by international groups such as the Global Anglican Future Conference, evangelicals have gained quite an influence. The majority of Anglican leadership and membership today is evangelical and lives in the Global South.

This in turn has transformed the conservative evangelicals within the Church of England in Britain—those who continued to revere the Doctor after 1966 and who in recent years have come to understand their prime identity no longer as territorial Anglicans but as *evangelicals*. Many vicars in movements such as Reform openly admit that they feel closer to their evangelical brothers in the FIEC than they do to their theoretical fellow denominational brethren in the Church of England.

Increasingly, these vicars are realizing for themselves that because their *prime* allegiance is to the gospel and to evangelical faith, they must now seek fellowship among the like-minded. And if that means their expulsion from the still territorially based Church of England—so be it!

As J. I. Packer has so rightly said to some of the Doctor's family, many evangelical Anglicans now believe that since territorial dioceses are man-made institutions, it is possible, for instance, to stay within the Anglican Communion, which is now majority evangelical, while operating outside of the territorial structures of the human-orientated diocesan system. Many faithful evangelical Episcopalian/Anglican churches in Canada, for instance, now affiliate with the strongly evangelical diocese of the Southern Cone in Latin America. And others, in both Britain and the United States, are now missionary extensions of dioceses in Africa that have stayed faithful to the Bible and to New Testament teaching.

To haul Dr. Lloyd-Jones into a discussion on the Anglican Communion in the twenty-first century, with the circumstances so radically changed since his death, is to be anachronistic. It is hard to know exactly what indeed he would have thought of the present day. But if any kind of speculation is allowed, one could argue that he has been proved right. Back in 1966 he could not have foreseen present-day circumstances, but events in the twenty-first century have proved him to be correct.

So-called "open evangelicals" still choose to actively participate in the denomination, learning, as they would put it, from the traditions of others. But in theologically conservative evangelical congregations, the name and works of Dr. Lloyd-Jones are often heard from many an Anglican pulpit, in expository sermons from Scripture based strongly on the model of the Doctor's book *Preaching and Preachers*.

In Britain, the "gospel partnerships" between biblically based evangelicals in the Church of England and their FIEC and similar brethren are restoring formerly broken links. Regardless of denominational affiliation, they come together as evangelicals to fight for the truths once delivered to the saints. In the eastern part of England, for example, Grace Baptist and Evangelical Anglican churches gathered together to hear Mark Dever, of Capitol Hill Baptist Church and cofounder of Together for the Gospel preach alongside the Archbishop of Sydney, Peter Jensen.

Oak Hill Theological College in London, always an evangelical institution, is now half FIEC and half Anglican, training people for Free Church ministry as well as for the Church of England. Bible-based evangelicals in the Church of England are finding their prime identity not within their denomination but outside it. Nearly half a century since the Doctor's address in London, countless evangelicals within the Church of England—and perhaps as many as 50 percent of those attending any kind of Anglican Church—are discovering that they agree with him. He has been vindicated, and by the views of evangelical Anglicans.

What they do next, and how they implement what they have found, is yet to be seen. But the imperatives of the gospel have changed everything, and that is surely nothing but good news.

IFES

We have used the term *evangelical* throughout this book. We think we know what we all mean by it—but do we? It would benefit us to look at how the Doctor himself defined it, specifically in the context of an organization to which he had a decades-long love and loyalty, the International Fellowship of Evangelical Students. People today often fail to recognize this part of his ministry, yet to him, and to millions around the world since 1945, IFES has been essential. Let us look at it to end this chapter on a note that, one hopes, truly does accentuate the positive!

In his "What Is an Evangelical?" addresses to IFES in 1971, Dr. Lloyd-Jones referred to the IFES Basis of Faith. It is one that he, along with others, spent much of his own time writing, in the years after the Second World War. He had initially met with evangelicals from other countries in 1939 with the idea of forming a global movement. His vision was that this movement would take in all the various evangelical student groups around the world, on the basis of clear gospel unity. Needless to say the Second World War rather got in the way over the next six years. But in 1945 they reconvened and began drafting the basis of faith.

Few people loved the old bases of faith and great catechisms of the past more than Dr. Lloyd-Jones, who knew and read them all. But as he points out in many of his books, they were written to deal with the specific instances of their own times. The Athanasian Creed, as he reminds us, deals with the Arian heresy, and the Augsburg Confession the recovery of biblical truth following the split with Rome.

In 1945, with the world exhausted by war, evangelical Christians from around the globe came in true biblical fellowship to see what they could do to form a genuinely international body of evangelical believers. The chairman was Martyn Lloyd-Jones, and he was to hold office as chairman or president until his retirement in 1971.

It is interesting that in the "What Is an Evangelical?" talks he discusses negatives as well as positives. That is, there are things that evangelicals *do* believe, but there are equally things that they reject and *do not* believe. Significantly, he felt that evangelicals *do not* believe in the sanctity of tradition.

He was referring specifically to the Roman Catholic Church, which puts tradition alongside Scripture as an equal source of authority. But he knew that evangelicals could be just as prone to relying on traditions of their own! No one was more devoted to the Puritans, to John Owen (whose entire works the Doctor owned in an early nineteenth-century reprint), and to the giants of the eighteenth century, such as Jonathan Edwards.

But remember that he was a Bible Calvinist, not a system

Calvinist! He knew that the magisterial confessions of the past were a sign of spiritual health, or as he put it, godly men of their particular generation reiterating the core truths of Scripture for the times in which God had placed them.

However, consider one group at the heart of evangelicalism today: Baptists. Many reading this will be Baptists and will know that many of the great Reformation creeds and formulae, to which we owe so much, are firmly paedobaptist in their theology. They also often presume a church-state link that is alien to the Baptist belief in the firm separation of church and state.

So we can learn an enormous amount from such creeds. But they were written by biblical Christians for other times responding to other issues. And they are man-made constructions, not the words of Scripture themselves.

So when the group of evangelicals, chaired by Dr. Lloyd-Jones, met together after the horrors of World War II, they created the IFES Basis of Faith.[10] What follows emerged over many sessions in the years 1945–1947. It is a clarion declaration of evangelical belief that has stood the test of changing times:

> IFES is founded on the central truths of biblical Christianity as outlined in the IFES doctrinal basis. IFES is a non-denominational organisation that brings together Christians from all cultures, languages and Christian traditions. Every four years the IFES Fellowship meets at World Assembly to reaffirm their commitment to the biblical truths expressed in our doctrinal statement.
>
> The IFES doctrinal basis shall be the central truths of Christianity, as revealed in Scripture, including:
>
> - The unity of the Father, Son and Holy Spirit in the Godhead.
> - The sovereignty of God in creation, revelation, redemption and final judgment.

---

[10] There have been only the smallest changes since 1945, those being approved by the late Robin Wells, a former member of the Westminster Chapel congregation, General Secretary of Universities and Colleges Christian Fellowship, and a friend of many of the Doctor's family.

- The divine inspiration and entire trustworthiness of Holy Scripture, as originally given, and its supreme authority in all matters of faith and conduct.
- The universal sinfulness and guilt of all people since the fall, rendering them subject to God's wrath and condemnation.
- Redemption from the guilt, penalty, dominion and pollution of sin, solely through the sacrificial death (as our representative and substitute) of the Lord Jesus Christ, the incarnate Son of God.
- The bodily resurrection of the Lord Jesus Christ from the dead and his ascension to the right hand of God the Father.
- The presence and power of the Holy Spirit in the work of regeneration.
- The justification of the sinner by the grace of God through faith alone.
- The indwelling and work of the Holy Spirit in the believer.
- The one holy universal Church which is the body of Christ and to which all true believers belong.
- The expectation of the personal return of the Lord Jesus Christ.[11]

The Doctor's only reservation (as noted in an address he delivered in 1971) was that he would substitute the word "sole" for "supreme" in relation to Scripture. But otherwise, this is a statement of evident evangelical belief, created in the ruins of a world in which approximately 80 million people had just been slaughtered in the worst war in history, but which is as relevant seventy years later today as it was then.

This is a doctrinal basis that Baptists, Methodists, Presbyterians, Episcopalians, and Pentecostals can all sign—*if they are evangelical.* Dr. Lloyd-Jones despised those who affirmed creeds with

---

[11] International Fellowship of Evangelical Students Basis of Faith, accessed September 12, 2014, http://ifesworld.org/en/our-beliefs.

"mental reservations," such as many liberals in denominations that still retained conservative bases of faith. But it would be hard for a nonevangelical to assent in any form to a doctrinal basis such as this one!

It is interesting that the IFES basis of faith is both exclusive and inclusive. Secondary differences do not and should not divide evangelicals. However, those who reject Scripture, who spurn the core truths of the cross and the resurrection, are necessarily excluded from the evangelical fold. IFES has always been interdenominational, with Lutherans, Baptists, and Pentecostals—Calvinists and Arminians—together in its ranks, united around the core tenets of the faith that they *do* hold in common.

This kind of evangelical association was surely closest to the heart of what Martyn Lloyd-Jones perceived Christ-centered, Bible-believing evangelical unity to be all about. Let us therefore not think of the Doctor in a negative way but in one that is wholly positive. The positive model he gave us, embodied by the IFES, is the one for which he should be remembered.

7

Life in the Spirit

THE DOCTOR AT HOME

Today we hear a lot about the family, and about family values. But what are these critical parts of life in *biblical* terms? For this, we can turn to one of Dr. Lloyd-Jones's best-loved books: *Life in the Spirit in Marriage, Home and Work: An Exposition of Ephesians 5:18 to 6:9*. It remains one of his most popular works, for the obvious reason that the family, the home, and where we work are at the center of our everyday lives, whoever we are or wherever (and whenever) we live. Many a newlywed couple has been given this book as a wedding present! We all have social and personal relationships and a job to keep the roof over our heads. How to deal with all this *as Christians* is at the heart of the Doctor's exposition from Ephesians. (For a description of his own family relationships, see my book, *Martyn Lloyd-Jones: A Family Portrait*.[1] He was such a content and devoted family man.)

In a very important sense, what he preached and wrote about the family, husband-wife relations, and issues of headship in the 1950s and '60s is central to how evangelicals perceive themselves

---

[1] Christopher Catherwood, *Martyn Lloyd-Jones: A Family Portrait* (Grand Rapids, MI: Baker, 1995).

in the twenty-first century and how they are thought of by out-siders, especially in the context of the culture wars in the United States. In the United States terms such as "family values" or being "pro-family" are symbols, emblematic of deeper social, cultural, and theological attitudes, and, as often as not, of political affiliation as well. They are the touchstones of how someone is judged—is she or he *pro-family*?

Life in the Spirit is a compilation of sermons that were preached in the early 1960s, that notorious decade in which centuries (if not millennia) of cultural and behavioral norms were overthrown in favor of the chaos and anarchy of the age of flower power, hippie-dom, and rebellion against all kinds of authority. In Britain the laws on issues such as divorce and homosexuality were altered in a hu-manistic direction. The era in which people still followed Christian morals, even if they did not believe in Christian truth, effectively came to an end. By the time the book was published in 1974, the "Woodstock Generation" and *Roe v. Wade* had brought the United States into the same essentially post-Christian era.

What the Doctor preached was entirely counterintuitive to the times in which he lived. What he said went completely against the *zeitgeist* of the permissiveness that surrounded him. Yet Westminster Chapel was packed every Sunday as he preached from Ephesians. His contemporaries kept on saying that to go against popular opin-ion would empty churches as modern people wanted "relevant" teaching acceptable to twentieth-century mores. Every Sunday he proved them utterly wrong! Popularity never worried him—what he always sought was to be faithful to Scripture, regardless of what *bien-pensant* opinion might say.

But what is also interesting is that the Doctor rejected all politi-cal solutions as inevitably failing to solve what he knew to be the root problem—the rejection of God's standards as part of the over-all rebellion against God's truth and way of salvation. The basic issue was, as always, *spiritual*. And therefore he dealt with matters as just that—the results of humanity's refusal to turn to God, putting self above all else, and reducing morals to whatever suits the individual rather than loving obedience to God in gratitude for salvation. Only Christ on the cross can solve the underlying moral issues of the time, since only the work of the Holy Spirit in a believer's soul can bring about inward moral change.

In this his sixth book based on his Ephesians sermon series, Dr. Lloyd-Jones starts by addressing the "New Life in the Spirit" rather than going straight to today's presentational issues of family, marriage, and raising children. Today we often begin with the family rather than with the root causes of why the family has so visibly disintegrated. (We should note that here "life in the Spirit" is different from the sometimes controversial topic of baptism with the Holy Spirit. Here he is talking about the indwelling of the Holy Spirit in all Christians rather than a separate and further experience of the Spirit.)

In truth, all Christian behavior is and should be the result of being born again, of being a new creation, of being redeemed by the completed work of Jesus upon the cross. Throughout his exposition of this part of Paul's epistle to the Ephesians, the Doctor reminds us of these core truths.

The Doctor's presumption is that theology precedes anything else, and that any action short of spiritual rebirth will fail. Without the inward basic change of conversion, sinful people do not change. So to him, to be "pro-family" was to believe in the basic unit of society created by God himself from the beginning of time. This is a *spiritual* definition. Fallen humanity might have different reasons for rejecting it, but in essence, opposing God's ordination is not so much a political stance but a human, sinful rebellion against the decrees of God. It is to put oneself above the laws of the Creator.

Since the 1960s issues involving the family have become politicized in many countries. This is true in the United States, with fifty or so years of overt societal rejection of the Bible's norms. It is also true of other parts of the world where the same spiritual decline has taken place.

I have not tried to invent "what would the Doctor think if he were alive today" responses to particular current events, many of which could not have been predicted in detail in his lifetime. *But biblical principles are eternal and remain ever the same.*

So while the Doctor would have been aware, both in the early 1960s when he preached these sermons and in the mid-1970s when they were published, of societal trends in the West, he thought in terms of scriptural verities rather than of reacting to outside events. God's truth is permanent. It was true in the first century when Paul wrote the epistle; it was true in the twentieth century when the Doctor engaged with it; and it is true for us in the twenty-first century. As a historian, Lloyd-Jones knew of the decadence of seventeenth-century Restoration England, during which many godly Puritans such as John Bunyan were imprisoned. He also knew of the debauchery of eighteenth-century Georgian London, where all the decadence we see in our own times was flaunted openly with the same degree that we see today. And nowhere in today's Western world is yet as utterly depraved as society was in Roman times, during which the apostle wrote his epistle. The expression of sin might change, but the fact of it, the rebellion against God and against his creation ordinances, remains the same.

In focusing on the spiritual, the Doctor knew that he was going against the *zeitgeist* of his day. But he knew that he expounded biblical truth. As he put it:

> So if the church is anxious that her teaching should permeate the life of society, the quickest and the shortest way to accomplish that is not to preach politics, is not to preach about social matters, is not to be forever protesting against this and that; it is to produce a larger number of Christians. And how is that done? By preaching the pure Gospel, by preaching a Gospel that can convert people. . . . Very many of our churches are empty today because so many preachers have preached nothing but sermons on politics and social matters. They have not been preaching the Gospel, and have not been converting men and

women; and so there are fewer and fewer Christians, and the "powers that be" ignore us and can afford to forget us entirely.[2]

As he continued in the same sermon:

It is idle to ask for this sort of conduct unless a man is already a possessor of the Holy Spirit. If I may so put it, you cannot live the life of the Kingdom of God until you have entered the Kingdom of God. You cannot share the life of the Kingdom of God without being a citizen of that Kingdom. . . . This modern teaching is a complete denial of the biblical doctrine of sin and of the depravity of the natural human heart.[3]

How true that is! "Family values" are the values of God's family, the church. How are people going to come to accept those values? They will do so by becoming part of God's family, the church—and that means *by becoming Christians.*

It is interesting that the Doctor, back in the 1960s, was aware that not everyone agreed with this. Again, we must not be side-tracked by twenty-first-century politics! Indeed, he did not deal *politically* with what concerned him. What worried him was what he perceived to be a lack of balance among godly evangelicals in the United States, a misdirected reaction to the increasing secularization they saw around them.

How does society change? It is through *conversion.* The Doctor had seen in his own life—in his childhood in London and in South Wales as a pastor—Christians attempting to introduce Christian moral behavior to non-Christian people without those same non-Christians becoming converted to new life in Jesus Christ. By the 1960s the very idea of Christian morals without belief in the faith that created them had become meaningless, and we live with the results today.

It is wonderful if our non-Christian friends and neighbors come to believe, for example, that "family values" are a nice ideal and

---

[2] Lloyd-Jones, *Life in the Spirit in Marriage, Home & Work: An Exposition of Ephesians 5:18 to 6:9* (Edinburgh: Banner of Truth, 1973), 30.
[3] Ibid., 32.

worth implementing. As the Doctor explicitly argued, the societal effects of the rejection of Christian moral values was already catastrophic in his time and patently obvious to everyone. Now in the twenty-first century, the results are incomparably worse, and in some way are obvious even to the most secular of sociologists and commentators.

Individual "decent" people might take note and want to emulate the family values that make Christians increasingly distinct from the collapsing moral order around them. That might be nice! But *spiritually* speaking, they are nice *non-Christians*. No one goes to heaven by accepting family values, but by accepting Jesus Christ as Savior and Lord. Values redeem nobody. Jesus alone does that, on the cross. Nice family values people are still destined for hell unless they are born again, since, as the Bible puts it rather starkly, we are all sinners (Rom. 3:23). All our righteousness is no more than filthy rags (Isa. 64:6), however kind we are to our elderly neighbors, to our old grandmother, or whatever family value one might choose.

THE DOCTOR AND MARRIAGE

We see this priority in the Doctor's discussion of marriage. To him marriage between Christians is innately different from a marriage, however happy, between two people who are not Christian. We cannot, as Christians, separate our own view of marriage from the nature of the relationship between God and his people, since that is the very analogy that Scripture itself employs.

> In telling wives and husbands how to behave towards one another [the apostle Paul] introduces the doctrine of the nature of the church and the relationship of the church to Christ. . . . Here in this most practical of sections, Paul suddenly introduces this tremendous doctrine of the nature of the church. . . . But what we must bear in mind . . . is that doctrine and practice are so intimately related that they cannot be separated. . . . [The] Christian view of marriage is a unique view; it is a view that is entirely different from every other view, it is a view that you only find in

the Bible. . . . In other words it comes to this; if we are not clear about the Lord Jesus Christ and the church, and the relationship of the church to Him, we cannot understand marriage. . . . You cannot understand marriage unless you are a Christian.[4]

Spiritually speaking, all this should be abundantly obvious! But in reaction to the increasing decadence and secularism around us, are we as twenty-first-century evangelicals in danger of putting the cart before the horse? We live in a society in which our values are those of an increasingly small minority, and much of the world around us is ever more alien. But wasn't that the case (even more so) of Roman society? The slaughter of the innocents in the arena surely makes anything we see today mild in comparison—nothing in Hollywood matches the Colosseum, where the deaths were very real indeed. Christians were an infinitesimally smaller minority than today. Yet, as the Doctor reminds us, the New Testament Epistles do not campaign against the murder of women and children by lions, though such atrocities were utterly contrary to the law of God. Rather, the Bible counsels Christians to put Christ first, to live lives of holiness and obedience to God, of such distinctiveness that the decadent world around could not help but notice.

THE DOCTOR AND FAMILY

Let us look in a bit more detail at what he actually said about the family.

He was in favor of headship, of what is now called a complementarian view of marriage, and of discipline for children. But the scriptural framework in which he operated should not be forgotten. Men should love their wives as Christ loved the church (Eph. 5:25). Almost all Christians acknowledge that in theory. But do we do so in practice? The Doctor was most concerned that Christian husbands should not forget the context of that command. Tyranny, of the kind that so besmirched the Victorian era, was something that

---

[4] Ibid., 92, 95, 97–98.

he abhorred. A Christian wife, similarly, should be submissive—but certainly not a doormat.

Those who knew the very happy marriage that the Doctor and his wife enjoyed saw not just the profound love that they had for each other but also their mutual respect. Martyn much admired Bethan's many gifts; she was a strong lady to whom the expression "doormat" could most assuredly never be applied! They did not converse about submission and headship; rather, they lived in harmony as each worked out how best to support the other. She saw her role as freeing her husband for Christian ministry. He, in turn, valued her insights and the freedom that she gave him to concentrate on his ministry.

Of course, one does not have to agree with every application that the Doctor personally practiced. For example, he never accepted an invitation to a social event to which his wife was not also asked. His motive was surely a good one—a Christian couple is a single unit, so to invite one half and not the other is a failure to acknowledge the bonds of marriage. But indeed there may be legitimate reasons why a husband alone would be invited to an event.

But even here the *principle* that the Doctor was expounding was a good one, whether one agrees with his particular application. He was horrified by the phenomenon of "evangelical widows": women whose husbands were so involved in so-called "Christian work" that they hardly ever saw their wives or children. This to him was wholly abhorrent, since a Christian husband has clear biblically mandated duties to his wife and children. Such behavior is entirely un-Christian, no matter what the supposedly spiritual motivation behind it might be. Although the Doctor was a zealous student of Christian biography, he would snort with indignation at more than a few eminent Christian leaders of the past who neglected their marital and paternal duties. In an age when workaholic behavior is the norm, in both Christian ministry and the secular workplace, the Doctor felt strongly we should never overlook our familial responsibilities.

On this topic, chapter 20 of *Life in the Spirit*, entitled "Balanced

Discipline," is so important. It is also emblematic of how the Doctor thought and expounded Scripture. He certainly believed in discipline in principle. As he reminds us, punishment for sin is at the heart of the atonement: Jesus was punished for our sins upon the cross. Dr. Lloyd-Jones would have had no truck whatsoever with those who today deny the doctrine of penal atonement, a view which to him would have been a denial of the gospel itself.

But, he argued, there should be a balance. The Victorians were far too harsh in their discipline of children, in the same way that current secular society (today as well as in the 1960s) is far too lax. "What is important," he wrote, "is that we must not fall into the error of reverting again from the present position to that other extreme which was equally wrong. And here, if we but follow the Scripture, we shall have a balanced view."[5]

When discussing the verse that commands fathers not to provoke their children to wrath, he explained:

> The ever-present danger is to react too violently. It is always wrong when our attitude is determined by another attitude which we regard as wrong. Our view should never result from a merely negative reaction. This principle is true not only with respect to this particular subject, but in many realms and departments of life. . . . Our position must always be determined positively by the Scriptures. We must not merely be reactionaries. And in this particular matter of discipline in the home, and of children, there is a very real danger that good Evangelical Christians, having seen clearly that the modern attitude is entirely and utterly wrong, and being determined not to accept it, may go to the other extreme and revert to the old Victorian idea. They therefore need the exhortation [not to provoke their children to wrath].[6]

As usual, a particular injunction—not provoking children to what he interpreted as resentment—is one which, because it is

---

5 Ibid., 276.
6 Ibid., 277.

Scripture-based, can be applied to all kinds of other issues as well. He counseled against being mere reactionaries. In a society that has rejected even the notion of Christian values, it is all too easy to react against the decadence that daily surrounds us. But (as we have seen elsewhere) our society today is mild in comparison with the greater horrors of first-century Roman life; films today sanitize ancient atrocities without thinking of the true gore of, for instance, watching people being ripped apart by wild animals for fun. Our moral climate today seems tame in comparison with Roman times.

We must note that the Doctor never presumed that the children of Christian parents would themselves automatically become Christians. His was a thoroughly Reformed interpretation of the Scriptures. How many parents are Reformed in theory but Arminian in practice, especially when it comes to their own children? One cannot, he demonstrates from the Bible, force a "decision" upon any child, since unless such a decision is a direct work of God, it is useless. Only the work of the Holy Spirit within someone can lead anyone to a true and saving faith in Jesus Christ.

In conclusion, the Doctor enables us to put our sorrows and woes regarding the onward march of secularization into a proper biblical perspective. Mankind, he repeated often in his sermons, is *sinful*. The natural response of humankind is to reject the message and ways of God. Such it has always been and will continue to be until the end of time. If we believe the Bible—and, in the case of evangelicals of Reformed persuasion, if we believe in total depravity—we should not expect anything else! The issues are spiritual, and the only remedy therefore must also be spiritual: the message of Christ upon the cross. It is a lesson that we, as twenty-first-century evangelicals, should never tire of learning.

8

Imagined Communities

LIFE AT THE CHAPEL AND IN HISTORY

One of the most influential academic books of recent years is one by the sociologist Benedict Anderson. *Imagined Communities* explained to many people back in the ethnic turmoil and conflicts of the 1990s how nations can imagine a past that changes how they behave in the present.[1] In September 2001 this became globally relevant, since the extremists of al-Qaeda wanted to recreate a mythic Islamic caliphate of a kind that never in fact existed. People have also imagined good communities, such as the Puritans' attempts to create a "godly commonwealth" in Massachusetts. In short, such an entity is an idealized version of the past to which we look back fondly and hope to see again in our own lifetimes.

When considering the Doctor, we can see two kinds of imagined communities. We will first examine the kind that existed during his thirty years at Westminster Chapel (and especially after the war ended, particularly 1945–1968). Second, we note his abiding love of history, of the stories of great revivals, and of the eras of the

---

[1] Benedict Anderson, *Imagined Communities: Reflections on the Origins and Spread of Nationalism*, rev. ed. (London: Verso, 2006).

Puritans and the godly giants of the eighteenth century, such as Whitefield and Edwards.

THE WESTMINSTER CHAPEL YEARS

On the twenty-fifth anniversary of his death, many old Westminster Chapel congregants met for a conference that looked back on their time there under the Doctor and his unique ministry. There were many tears and fond recollections, with the phrase "those were great days" frequently uttered. And for those sharing such memories, it was true.

When the Doctor retired because of ill health in 1968, the congregation never again saw the kind of numbers that were present in his time. The Chapel, under the leadership of neither of his first two successors, had nothing like the numbers that the Doctor was familiar with seeing Sunday after Sunday during his tenure, especially post-1945.

Does this matter? And what does this tell us about similar churches today, where one has to arrive early to obtain a seat, and where there is a similar sense of community based around a preacher of particular unction and great spiritual preaching power, but who is, like the Doctor himself, only mortal?

There is no doubt that Westminster Chapel in the Doctor's era fits exactly into what one might describe as the Andersonian criteria, in which we idealize the past. Westminster Chapel was in no sense a typical local church. And the Doctor's own writings clearly show that it was an awkward building; to him the fact that it was nicknamed a "nonconformist Cathedral" was a source of sorrow and not something in which to boast. As he pointed out, without the aid of a microphone, preaching in so vast and cavernous a building placed a severe physical strain on the preacher, and several of his predecessors wilted under the task.

Furthermore, as he also made plain, most of the previous ministers of the Chapel were not in any sense evangelical, certainly not in the way that could be applied either to him or to his immediate predecessor, G. Campbell Morgan. And theologically, in terms of Reformed theology preached as logic on fire, Dr. Lloyd-Jones was very much a first, with none of his predecessors fitting such a mold.

One of the unique things about a day at the Chapel is that people stayed all day, from around ten thirty on a Sunday morning until around eight on a Sunday night. Sunday school did not run parallel with the Sunday morning service as happens in many British churches, nor was it something to attend before or after a morning service, as is common in many a church in the United States. Rather, it was in the afternoon, and was for all ages, from tiny children to the very elderly.

So a typical Sunday would look something like this:

1. Food placed in the church ovens.
2. Morning service.
3. Lunch in one of the church halls.
4. Sunday school for all ages.
5. Tea time in one of the church halls.
6. Prayer meeting.
7. Evening service.
8. Coffee time in one of the church halls.

One could spend around ten hours in the church, although in many cases the break between lunch and Sunday school often entailed a walk around St. James's Park, a visit to an art gallery, or even (for those able to find resting places) a brief snooze.

Much of this pattern arose because of the wartime need to stay in one location, since travel on the train, bus, or underground was unwise during the war. But what arose as a temporary and necessary expedient became established as a habit, and remained so for many years afterward, including (so far as I am aware) on a more limited scale the years after the Doctor's retirement.

If you spend ten hours every Sunday with people, you get to know them rather well, especially if, as evangelical Christians, you have the most important thing of all in common with each other. Countless people met their future spouse at the Chapel, so friendships forged there were life-changing events. As happens in any church, there were those who stayed decades (there are still people at Westminster Chapel who first started to attend during the Second World War), and those passing through London as students or for job purposes who were very active during their stay but who moved on elsewhere as life progressed.

I think it is true to state that the core nucleus was large, bigger than most churches at the time. And so a group was formed that spent many hours together week by week for decades. Today at the Chapel, under the strongly theologically Reformed ministry of Greg Haslam, there are fourth-generation families, the great-grandchildren of people whose forebears first started coming to the church in the Doctor's time. Many of the second generation married each other and now have grandchildren of their own.

But this was a community based not on a geographic area, but on a shared desire to hear the weekly preaching of one of the greatest expositors of the twentieth century. People came miles from the north and south of London and from all over Greater London, which is itself one of the world's largest urban conurbations; in the Doctor's time it was one of the most populous cities on the planet.

So we should not idealize the past. Westminster Chapel was a wonderful place, but it was very much the kind of "imagined community" about which Anderson writes.

Those who remember it look back at the fellowship they had then as a wonderful era. But some of those close to the Doctor feel that it was also a *unique* time, created by God for a particular purpose and not capable of being replicated today. Thousands of people passed through the Chapel in those days, many of them from overseas, and they were able to make a huge difference from having been under the Doctor's ministry whether they went on to churches in the United Kingdom or in faraway countries. It was not in any sense a typical congregation, and it was, by its very definition, created in wartime circumstances that thereafter ceased to be normal, and by the preaching of an exceptionally gifted expositor. Many feel that they were "good days," but good days for a purpose, for the wider benefit of the global evangelical church. When his sermons began to be published, millions of Christians around the world were able to benefit from the unique preaching ministry that took place there during that twenty-three-year peacetime period.

This is an important perspective, since the nature of the ministry has come under criticism by those who feel, correctly, that Westminster Chapel was not a typical local church. In the terms of how we would expect an evangelical church to be run today, that was indeed the case. One of the distinguishing features of evangelical churches in our time is the existence of neighborhood home groups, of members of the congregation in a smaller local area studying the Bible and praying together week by week. Some churches integrate their study passage with the sermons, others study books of the Bible, but all are based on the idea of active members of the church meeting together regularly in someone's home to study God's Word in greater depth as well as to pray for one another and the church.

Some attempts were made in the Doctor's time to do this, but logistics made it difficult—it is hard for people forty miles or more apart to come together on a weekday, and long-distance travel negates the idea of *neighborhood* study. Home groups (or small group Bible studies) also act as smaller fellowship units and as pastoral support groups, since the average weekly meeting usually has time set aside for prayer concerns and practical help and advice. One can do this with a group of twelve to fifteen Christians who live near each other, but not really with a church of two thousand spread all over a huge geographical area.

Obviously the communal lunch, tea, and coffee times at Westminster Chapel replicated in one sense some of the aspects of home groups. And friends would see each other on Saturdays or holidays. But the Bible study times were held on Sundays and in much larger groups, meeting on the church premises.

If one takes the view of those close to the Doctor that his ministry time at the Chapel was an unrepeatable special time of ministry—of equipping the saints worldwide for a generation—then the pattern that existed under him is one that can indeed be defended *so long as we remember that the circumstances in which that era existed were unique.*

It should be said that those who have criticized the Doctor *specifically* fail to take into account the wider point that similar things can be said of any megachurch. When there is an especially God-gifted preacher, such as Lloyd-Jones (and other London contemporaries of his, such as John Stott or R. C. Lucas, whose respective churches were equally filled to the rafters), it is understandable that those who can travel there will want to do so. One could hardly have asked All Souls Church, Langham Place, under Dr. Stott or Westminster Chapel under Dr. Lloyd-Jones to ask people how many miles they had come, and if it was too great a distance then ask them to leave! Wanting to hear a great preacher is only human.

The same applies to the myth that the Doctor was a dictator. To those who knew him well, the very notion that he even could be a dictator is entirely ludicrous!

When he tried to take Westminster Chapel from the Congregational Union into the Fellowship of Independent Evangelical Churches, there was considerable and very vocal stiff opposition among many in the congregation itself, which was, one must remember, a democracy. The Doctor eventually succeeded in his quest, but not without much animated discussion at church meetings, at which all opinions were heard and at which the members had a vote.

Furthermore, the deacons were far from spineless! The point about an imagined community such as Westminster Chapel is that it was a church that existed to hear the preaching of *Martyn Lloyd-Jones.* The people who came to it did so because in the main they agreed with him *already.* Many of the deacons were men who had fought bravely during the Second World War. These were not supine men cowed by a dictator into doing his will. Rather, they were men who were there out of theological conviction, and thus agreed with the Doctor and his basic precepts not out of intimidation but because of their *prior* views. Had they not already agreed with him, they would never have come to the Chapel in the first place.

This again is not so much a Lloyd-Jones issue, but one of large churches that exist because of the very special—and thus unusual—preaching of an individual given great unction from God. And the Chapel was not a personality cult; the whole idea of wearing a black Geneva gown was to hide the man and give prominence not to the messenger but to the message.

But of course such churches are not the norm. There is much to be said for today's evangelical emphasis on church planting. Likewise, effective discipleship and mutual accountability are emphasized much more strongly now than in the past. There comes a time when a church is simply too big for everyone to know each other. Many prospering evangelical churches are located in areas where they can replicate in an area of the town or countryside not so far away where gospel ministry is thin on the ground and needs encouragement. Similarly, while small group Bible studies are an excellent way to get to know fellow church members well and be of practical and prayerful assistance, training in Godly discipleship is also a wise move. So many new Christians come from utterly unchurched backgrounds, with no knowledge of Christian practice and behavior, that such effective discipleship is more necessary today than ever.

If all two thousand people who attended Westminster Chapel on a Sunday (and because some people came to only one service, attendance could have been around three thousand or more) stayed all day, they would never have *all* fit in the halls where people had lunch or tea. Therefore, in addition to the core group who stayed all day and had close fellowship, the Chapel had a large fringe. Some of these were people who attended their own church in the morning and the Chapel at night, and so were Christians well looked-after by their own congregations. But others, as I often hear, were in effect passengers; they simply attended and never truly came under the proper discipline of a church (in the terms that, say, the 9Marks model feels are essential for proper spiritual growth and discipleship). And the staff at the Chapel was not large enough to deal with such people—compared to today's churches, the full-time salaried staff at Westminster was miniscule, with much of the work being done by devoted volunteers who had jobs elsewhere during the week.

No church pattern is perfect, because all are comprised of human beings. For instance, while the 9Marks model works effectively in the American churches where it is used, it may not be universally applicable in other countries or cultures. It is, however, an example of how godly ministers of the gospel have thought through the issues and come up with a possible way forward.

But the advantage of such structures is that one can have a strongly evangelical church that is not dependent on the unction and special preaching power of a single God-anointed individual. There are very few like Martyn Lloyd-Jones in any given century. But there are countless godly, Bible-centered, Christ-proclaiming faithful preachers who expound the Word of God week in week out, year by year, whom God uses greatly in their own congregations even though the wider world has never heard of them.

We looked at the vexing subject of music in chapter 5. The Chapel had an organist, but, as we have seen, no choir, something that was compensated for by the corporate and enthusiastic singing of the two thousand and more people in the congregation on a typical Sunday.

The Doctor led everything himself. He knew that music could become a source of pride and competition that was wholly worldly. Nonetheless, other churches that had equally high a view had different practice, such as All Souls Church, Langham Place, just down the road from the Chapel.

Christians often differ from each other very strongly on such matters, and perhaps will continue so to do well into the future. New thinking emerges all the time. Perhaps an extract from the *9Marks Journal* might be a possible pointer to a biblical theology of how to conduct a church service.

Discerning what biblical teaching on worship [sic] takes some finesse, since Scripture nowhere presents us with, for example, a complete, confessedly normative "order of service." But there are some commands in the New Testament which are pretty plainly binding on all churches. That the churches at Ephesus and Colossae were both commanded to sing (Eph. 5:18–19, Col. 3:16), and the Corinthian church is referred to as singing (1 Cor. 14:26), suggests that all churches are supposed to sing. That Paul commanded Timothy to read and preach Scripture in a letter designed to instruct Timothy about how the church is to conduct itself (1 Tim. 3:15, 4:14) suggests that reading and preaching Scripture are God's will not just for that one church, but for every church.[2]

The Doctor always chose the hymns himself. This makes sense considering that worship music should lead one into the meaning of the text, reflecting both words and mood. A rousing hymn or song followed by a reflective sermon creates a clash, so the words and music of the hymns that are chosen should tie in with the sermon that is to follow.

Singing and Bible reading were both present at Westminster Chapel services. The Doctor's prayers were at the heart of any Sunday as well. He would often pray at length, not just for the message but for the church itself, the universal church, and the state of the world, which, during the Cold War, was often precarious. Many people remember the Chapel as much for the Doctor's prayers as for his preaching, and the two were closely interlinked. He would always pray *extempore*, although he prepared his prayers as well as his sermons. Those who heard him often were especially aware of the presence of God when he prayed. Both he and the congregation really were speaking to God together.

However, he did all this by himself—only the reading of announcements by the church secretary introduced someone else into the pulpit. His pastoral assistants, such as Iain Murray and Herbert

---

[2] Bobby Jamieson, "Biblical Theology and Corporate Worship," *9Marks Journal* (Summer 2014), http://www.9marks.org/journal/biblical-theology-and-corporate-worship.

Carson, were not there to preach. It is remarkable that so large a church had so few staff. A leading evangelical church not far from London today has, for example, four preachers (the pastor and three other full-time pastoral/preaching staff) and a full-time team of over twenty people, and that congregation is just under half the size of the Chapel in the Doctor's time.

In British churches, especially in the Free Churches, the pattern at Westminster Chapel was often the norm back in that era, as it was in many churches in the United States. The minister really had to do everything at the Sunday service. In other parts of typical church life, such as afternoon Sunday school, much reliance was placed on enthusiastic volunteers.

But whether that should be a model for evangelical churches in our own time is another matter. Obviously no two congregations have the same financial resources, and what one church can afford would strain the budget of another. Furthermore, if one does not believe in the distinction between clergy and laity that evolved over centuries—the Bible clearly points to the priesthood of *all believers*, as rediscovered at the Reformation—there is plenty of scope for those who, like at the Chapel, wish to help as part of their Christian service. But the "one-man band" is not a scriptural pattern either, and nowhere does the Bible stipulate the number of teaching elders (with the pastor/teacher gift) allowed in any one congregation. Furthermore, churches with a plurality of teaching elders are not so dependent upon the health or longevity of any one individual—the rapid decline in numbers at the Chapel after the Doctor had to retire being an illustration of this point.

Once again, one can say that the Doctor was a unique individual for a particular time, and that it is the eternal message of Scripture as faithfully proclaimed there that can be our role model, rather than its particular form of music or ministry.

In addition, we tend to think that if there are not many famous globally distinguished preachers, then the church is in a bad state. Surely that is far from the case! God blesses the faithful, not the successful, and the books and sermons of Dr. Lloyd-Jones himself are filled with examples both from his own time and from history of those who gave their lives preaching the good news of Jesus Christ even to the tiniest gathering of listeners whom God nonetheless used and blessed. It is the world that lauds size and outward success, not the Scriptures.

THE DOCTOR'S LOVE OF HISTORY

We now come to the Doctor's love of history. He was forever telling his congregation to "read the biographies" and to study the history of the church, of how God has dealt with his people throughout the centuries, and, in particular, during great times of blessing and revival.

Dr. Lloyd-Jones chose to be buried with his wife's family, the Phillipses, rather than with his own. Evan Phillips (his wife's grandfather) had seen and experienced the revival of 1859. This event was in fact transatlantic, reaching America as well. Bethan Lloyd-Jones had witnessed the Welsh Revival of 1904–1905; her father sent her from London to Wales so she could to see it for herself. The chapel and graveyard where Martyn and Bethan Lloyd-Jones are buried, along with many of her ancestors, had been the scene of many of the great events both of 1859 and 1905, and the symbolism of the Doctor being buried there was thus enormous. (His son-in-law Fred Catherwood is now buried in the same place.)

He did not witness the wonderful events of 1904–1905 himself, and he never throughout the rest of his life saw the revival in Britain for which he so longed (although many revivals took place elsewhere during his lifetime). He preached a sermon series in 1959 at Westminster Chapel on the subject of revival, one of the rare times when he gave thematic sermons from Scripture rather than his usual practice of exposition through a whole book.[3]

No one was a greater enthusiast than Dr. Lloyd-Jones, and his excitement at the great works of God throughout history was

---

[3] These sermons were published as *Revival* (Wheaton, IL: Crossway, 1987).

infectious. He never looked at events in isolation, since he would also read in detail the background secular history to the period that he was studying. The fruits of his research and hard work often came out at the annual conference centered around the Puritans, initially in collaboration with J. I. Packer, a fellow enthusiast, and after 1966 under a similar but different remit. Several of the Doctor's descendants have gone on to study history (now including great-grandchildren), so his zeal has been transforming.

Inevitably, his view of history and his research methodology have come under discussion. In particular, discussion has arisen since the publication of Puritan specialist John Coffey's academically acclaimed chapter in the book *Engaging with Martyn Lloyd-Jones*. Coffey is an active evangelical in the Reformed and separated tradition, which the Doctor himself so passionately believed in.

Two questions have arisen.

First, what was the Doctor's actual purpose in studying history, and how does what he was aiming to do tie in with academic practice, arguably a quite separate discipline from what Dr. Lloyd-Jones was doing in his historical lectures?

Second, how does the Doctor's interest in history fit into the imagined community idea? For there is a case for saying that evangelicals, in looking at the past, are seeing more of an ideal to be emulated rather than an actual past that really occurred, which can have all sorts of consequences. (Commentators note this too fits in perfectly with the Anderson critique.)

I work from Professor Coffey's former College in Cambridge and trained in the same history faculty. I know this place from which academic critique of the Doctor comes. No one on a personal or spiritual level is more loyal to Dr. Lloyd-Jones than Professor Coffey himself. But it is vital to remember that the academic discipline of a university-trained historian is altogether different from that of a pastor whose calling is to build up God's people and to edify the church.

On the nature of academic discourse, Cambridge is far less influenced by postmodernism than many other humanities faculty. As Sir Richard Evans, the Welsh recently retired Regius Professor of History has put it, if we allow postmodernism and refuse to "privilege a narrative," then we have to give equal status to the Nazi "narrative" as to the Jewish.[4]

However, the main aim of academic historians is an objective exploration and understanding of the past. To write in a partisan way—except on issues such as the utter depravity of Nazi ideology—is not encouraged. Both sides of an argument have to be explored, and as many sources as possible investigated and discussed.

The Doctor was a preacher not an academic, although he greatly enjoyed the works of university historians, especially that of the doyen of Puritan studies of his time, the Marxist but profoundly Puritan-sympathetic Oxford historian Christopher Hill. When Dr. Lloyd-Jones spoke at the Puritan conference or lectured to a packed Westminster Chapel in 1967 to celebrate the 450th anniversary of Luther nailing the ninety-five theses to the door in Wittenberg, he was aiming to edify his congregation, not to provide a university discourse.

From an academic viewpoint, many of his talks broke all the normal rules on objectivity or in the selection of material. Many of the Puritans contemporaneous to his own particular heroes (such as John Owen) had fought to stay *inside* the Church of England, with the view of reforming it rather than leaving it. University historians would have looked at Puritans in both categories, since up until the great expulsion of the godly by Charles II in 1662 the Established Church continued to have many Puritans within its ranks. One of these was Richard Baxter. It is perhaps no coincidence that one of the eminent evangelical experts on Baxter is J. I. Packer, an evangelical in the Reformed mold who has stayed within the Anglican Communion rather than depart from it. In choosing to concentrate on Owen, one of the most outstanding evangelicals Britain has ever produced, but a firm Independent and separatist, the Doctor was

---

[4] Richard Evans, *In Defence of History* (London: Granta Books, 1997).

thus concentrating on a man whose ecclesiology was very much after his own heart.

To hear stories of revival, to see God still at work as mightily as ever, is to warm the Christian heart. In recent years Collin Hansen's *A God-Sized Vision* has reminded us of the extraordinary revivals in our own lifetimes, some since the Doctor's death in 1981, that truly encourage Christians today.[5] In 2014, there were more Christians in China than members of the Communist Party—well over one hundred million and possibly far more. Most of this growth has occurred during a kind of persecution not seen since the days of the early church, and God has been most wonderfully and miraculously at work. Dr. Lloyd-Jones was right: there is nothing like reading about revival to stir the soul and to encourage the believer.

Revival is, however, as the Doctor so rightly reminds us, a special work of God. It is not the norm. We have to be faithful where we are; one of the things that Dr. Lloyd-Jones pointed out often is that God still blesses and uses his people even in the most discouraging of circumstances and hostile environments. Western Christians have for long been complacent, but while the depth of actual persecution that we in the West are increasingly suffering might be exaggerated, there is no question that aggressive secularism is making life harder for evangelicals who are serious about the Bible. We do not face persecution on the scale suffered by our brothers and sisters in Christ during the years of the Cultural Revolution in China. But a general hostility or active indifference to the things of God and to a Christian stand on key moral issues is growing all the time. Being a Christian is certainly no longer part of the *zeitgeist* of the twenty-first century.

The other advantage of reading about revival is that it reminds us of how gloriously God is at work all over the world. We can become very parochial in our outlook and think that our own situation, whether good or bad, is the norm for Christians everywhere. As we now see, with the amazing spread of biblical Christianity in

---

[5] Collin Hansen and John Woodbridge, *A God-Sized Vision* (Grand Rapids, MI: 2010).

the Global South, this is far from being the case, since God is at work in contexts and cultures utterly different from our own. In that sense we need the message of revivals more than ever before.

So we can say that in the context in which he was lecturing about the past, the Doctor's main aim and purpose was to help nurture mature Christian growth among believers, not to give peer-reviewed academic treatises. History demonstrates how God has worked in the past. If Christians ignore the past, we can endlessly try to reinvent the wheel. We end up making the same mistakes that many a well-meaning but misguided Christian has made before us.

There is no question but that Dr. Lloyd-Jones, although he used the very latest academic research of his time, was highly selective in the models he chose and partisan in relation to the past. But we should not forget that he was a pastor, not a professor.

But out of the hands of someone of the Doctor's erudition and pastoral instincts, we Christians can easily invent our own imagined communities, and in a way that damages us as evangelicals today.

As the Doctor reminds us, revival is in the sovereign will and power of God. We cannot demand it, but only beg God to have mercy upon us and send it. And if we look on revival as something that happened only in the past, we forget that it is happening *now*. It is taking place in countries where there has perhaps not been a large and long-standing Christian witness, and in which the majority of the population are naturally far more open to the existence of spiritual realities and battles than we are in the secular and increasingly atheistic West. Just look at the extraordinary development of evangelical Christianity in Africa (where there were hardly any Christians pre-1900) or in Latin America (where Protestantism was virtually unknown). The Global South is now at the heart of evangelical Christianity.

Fascination with revival can become escapism if directed increasingly far into the past, a kind of nostalgia in which we imagine things were far better then than they are now.

It is vital for me as a British author not to comment too much on the internal culture wars of the United States. But on this issue there is perhaps not much difference between evangelicals in the United Kingdom and those in the United States. We look back to an age in which our respective nations were "Christian," when the Word of God was officially respected. We sometimes even go so far as to say that we lived in a "Christian country." We have a kind of historical Christian nostalgia for a bygone age or an imagined community that existed then and which we would love to see restored today.

For all his reverence for history and love of revivals, and however selective his choice of examples from past glories, the Doctor never endorsed this idealistic view of the past—and with excellent Bible-centered theological good reason. He certainly did not believe that England—or even Wales—was a Christian country. His knowledge of church history taught him the same about the United States; we see this in the magisterial work by Cotton Mather *The Great Works of Christ in America* (originally titled *Magnalia Christi Americana*).[6]

It was clear by Mather's time that the spiritual zeal of the founding fathers of New England was departing, and that the descendants had none of the depth of their forefathers. And this should not surprise us. God has no grandchildren, and being of even the godliest ancestry does not save us. The Half-Way Covenant of 1662 (formulated the year before Mather was born) showed that a godly commonwealth consisting only of Christians was in effect impossible because the children and grandchildren of the Puritan founders were, by any proper spiritual analysis, not Christians themselves.

And one should not forget that states such as Virginia were founded by far-from-godly cavaliers, entirely for money, who had nothing to do with Puritan spiritual zeal. It was the deist and far-from-Christian Thomas Jefferson who prevented godly Baptists and others in Virginia from being persecuted by the Episcopalian establishment when he introduced religious liberty in 1777 (and

---

[6] Cotton Mather, *The Great Works of Christ in America*, 2 vols., repr. of 1852 ed. (Edinburgh: Banner of Truth, 1979).

enacted in 1786). Much of the United States therefore has very secular foundations, as far from the ideals of the Puritans of New England as one can imagine.

American exceptionalism is of course a well-attested historical phenomenon, and when the United States has come to the rescue of an endangered world, as it did in 1917 and in 1941, the very cause of freedom itself is a profound reason for gratitude to the United States and the values for which it stands. In 1941 the Doctor was among countless Christians thanking God for the entry of the United States into the war.

But when we look at issues *biblically* and in *spiritual* terms, we surely see a very different picture. God's people are not a nation in the geographical sense, but in a global and entirely spiritual sense. All his children throughout the world are equally his people wherever they are politically or geographically. God's new covenant nation are *Christians*. This includes those living in countries in which Christians are persecuted, and which politically might be quite hostile to the United States. The People's Republic of China, with its 100 million-plus Christians is perhaps a good example.

So as the Puritans of New England (with the Half-Way Covenant of 1662) and the Puritan rulers of Britain (from 1649–1660, under the Commonwealth and Protectorate of Oliver Cromwell and his son Richard) discovered, one simply cannot establish a "Christian country," however desirable one might think such an outcome would be. By biblical definition there can be no such thing, as God's chosen people are no longer a nation but a church, and a church that is global in its membership as God calls to himself those from every nation under the sun.

The concept of a Christian nation thus fits classically into the model of Anderson's imagined communities. It is an ideal, a dream of what we think existed in the past and would like to see replicated in our own time, but for which, as Christians, we know surely will not happen this side of eternity. In heaven we really will be in God's perfect kingdom. But on the other side of the divide, we are

Christians living in a very fallen world, not in need of man-made solutions but of Jesus Christ as Savior and Lord.

In 2012 a leading evangelical pastor got in trouble with many fellow evangelicals for saying that a Mormon candidate for the presidency could not, *spiritually speaking*, be the answer to all of America's woes. He came under enormous attack for this. But surely, when he quoted the Doctor's sermon series on Ephesians, he had a point. As Lloyd-Jones says, "To expect Christian behavior from people who are not Christian betokens a colossal ignorance of sin and its ways as they are revealed in the Bible."[7]

To witness the moral decline of a nation is a dreadful thing to behold, and for Christians in Britain, the United States, and other places in which Christian modes of behavior were once respected and are now ignored, it is a tragedy. But the point, as the Doctor never tired of saying, is that *such people are not Christians*. Of course they behave in a selfish and degenerate way; that is how, when left to themselves, non-Christians normally behave. What we have now is a society that, having rejected Christian doctrine in one generation, now utterly repudiates Christian morality as well. It is exactly what the apostle Paul describes in the beginning of his epistle to the Romans. We are returning to the kind of non-Christian society that existed before the birth of the church in the first century. It is of course tragic to be in such a generation, but it is also not at all surprising.

The Doctor therefore lived, for all his love of the past, in the real world. It is possible to argue that he was too pessimistic or perhaps not as supportive of those Christian laity who believed that faithful witness in the secular world—as seen by Wilberforce with the slave trade or Shaftesbury with child labor—was part of Christian witness.

In the Reformed world Francis Schaeffer certainly had an alternative and thoroughly evangelical paradigm of faithful Christian engagement with "the culture." But when one contrasts the hope-

---

[7] I am grateful to my mother (the Doctor's elder daughter, Elizabeth) for this quote.

fulness of many evangelicals in the 1980s with the despair more usually expressed in our own day, one has to ask whether the Doctor, with his more pessimistic outlook, was in fact right after all.

Let us therefore leave the dream worlds of our imagined communities and seek to save those who are lost. Our nation may not change, but millions of individual lives might. It might be costly, as countless thousands of martyred Christians in Nigeria or imprisoned believers in China have discovered. But it is the undisputed good news of Jesus Christ and him crucified that we are preaching, as the Doctor did throughout his adult life. Above all, this is the way of Scripture, of the apostles and the early church, and it is the path which we should all follow.

9

Pro-Millennial and
Other Notions

One of the leading evangelical churches in the United States, Capitol Hill Baptist Church in Washington, DC, has declared itself "promillennial." Is this a fourth position on that perpetually vexing question of what to believe on the second coming of Jesus Christ? Or is it a proclamation that this is an issue upon which evangelicals can legitimately differ? Whichever of the many end-times interpretations turns out to be the right one, at least we can all lovingly agree with each other that he is most certainly coming back, and he is coming back in judgment.

Increasingly, denominations and denominational thinking is becoming something of the past, as evangelicals are returning to Bible-based unity as opposed to man-made divisions. One could argue that denominations are a by-product of the Reformation, since we as Protestants reject the whole notion of a pope.

The very notion of a "state church" that has so dogged Christianity ever since the fourth century is still with us in many countries. Emperor Constantine made a deal with church leaders that the state had the right to interfere in the internal affairs of the church. We have, for example, the Church of England, the Lutheran churches in nations such as Denmark and Norway, and the Roman Catholic

Church, which remains the official representative of Christianity in many places. But as the Doctor pointed out, there is no biblical foundation for a state church. Furthermore, he reminded us, the Erastian idea that the state can control the church is as unbiblical as the notion the popes had in the Middle Ages that they could exercise superior authority over nations.

The church, therefore, is the people of God, and the kingdom of God is the rule of God upon earth.

It is of course natural that we form denominational groups. And it is clear, looking at the Doctor's work, that he recognized the scope for disagreement among evangelicals on all kinds of issues. The millennium, baptism, church government: all of these are contentious matters upon which God's people legitimately differ one from the other.

Today the concept of a Reformed Baptist appears to be a new one, although historically many Baptists held to both the doctrines of grace and to a Baptist view of baptism.[1] In Britain the doctrinally Reformed Grace Baptist (formerly Strict Baptist) denomination is centuries old. Now there are countless Baptists within existing Baptist denominations who hold strongly to the doctrines of grace and what one might describe as a Reformed view of God's sovereignty at work in salvation.

BAPTISM

Dr. Lloyd-Jones was never in any formal sense a Baptist. Westminster Chapel was in the Congregational Union and then later in the Fellowship of Independent Evangelical Churches. The Doctor has, with much merit, been called the last of the great Welsh Calvinistic Methodists, which is in fact a Presbyterian denomination and which holds to a paedobaptist covenant view of baptism similar to that held by many of the magisterial Reformers of the sixteenth century.

Since what the Doctor said to whom in which group is the

---

[1] For an accessible website on the history of reformed Baptists, see "The Church Hall of History: The Baptists," accessed September 14, 2014, http://www.spurgeon.org/~phil/baptist.htm.

source of endless controversy among his cessationist followers in Britain, such matters are best avoided as a distraction. So the key point here is that in the early 1950s at Westminster Chapel, in his Great Doctrines series to the Friday-nighters, he expounded both the biblical nature of Reformed theology and a *Baptist* interpretation of baptism, again based on his view of Scripture.

So was Dr. Lloyd-Jones a Baptist? Denominationally, the answer is no. But did he feel that believer's baptism was the Scriptural pattern? The answer to that is clearly yes. However, it is clear from Great Doctrines that he was unconvinced on the necessity of full immersion, and at Westminster Chapel neither he nor his successor Glyn Owen had baptismal pools; these came when Owen's successor, R. T. Kendall, came to the Chapel. Indeed, in one of his characteristic asides, the Doctor went so far as to insist that demanding a particular mode was heretical!

He also saw baptism as a seal, a way in which God confirms that someone has united with God's people, through Christ's death on the cross. Today we often see baptisms as wonderful opportunities for evangelism, with the person being baptized using the occasion to witness to non-Christian friends and family. To Dr. Lloyd-Jones this was not the main purpose of baptism.

There is no reason why we cannot see baptisms in both ways, as the inner purpose for the believer and the outer one of witness to an unbelieving world are surely not contradictory. And today, as we have seen elsewhere, many an evangelical church in the Anglican Communion now practices believer's baptism by immersion for the many in the congregation who have been converted to Christian faith as adults. So today many Baptists are Reformed and many Anglicans are Baptist in practice, and thankfully all are within an evangelical understanding of Christian faith.

CHURCH GOVERNMENT

In terms of church government, the Doctor was, like the FIEC, very much in the independent tradition of the Reformation. To be *independent* meant that each church was self-governed. A giant of the seventeenth-century English Puritans, John Owen, was one of Lloyd-Jones's leading inspirations. Independence meant that a church would not be responsible for heresy elsewhere, which would always, the Doctor felt, be the case with any kind of denominational loyalty—not just with the Anglicans, but equally with Presbyterians and any other kind of human-made institution that could go astray.

Sadly, of course, local independent churches can go wrong too. His own Westminster Chapel had been far from evangelical before his time, except under his immediate predecessor, G. Campbell Morgan. Many controversial things took place there in later years after Dr. Lloyd-Jones's death; one cannot even guarantee one's own church. We can also think of groups or universities or other godly founded institutions that have sadly lost their way. But he was right to say that denominations are often strange alliances of the evangelical and the middle-of-the-road and the outright liberal and the quasi-Catholic. How many evangelicals are in Methodist churches today? Yet look how wonderfully that group was founded, in the midst of revival. Continuity in faithfulness is surely a gift from God alone. If we have that continuity, it never comes from our own efforts but it is granted by God's love and mercy.

COMMUNION

Communion, or the Lord's Supper, is another area of disagreement among the faithful. The Doctor obviously did not ascribe to the Catholic view, but neither did he hold to the view of Luther, a classic compromise doctrine upon which the Doctor felt that Luther had buckled. Nor was Dr. Lloyd-Jones a Zwinglian, regarding communion purely as a commemoration. Instead he felt that the Westminster Confession had correctly interpreted Paul's epistle to the Romans, that communion is not just a sign but a seal, a promise from God. Just as a married man has a wedding ring, so too communion is what the Doctor called a "seal of grace."

In other words, the Doctor was not a man who could be pigeonholed! The quest for the correct interpretation of Scripture took him, as always, to a position that was Christ-centered and Bible-based, not to the human-made formulae of which denominational statements and creeds are based.

THE END TIMES

One of the great ironies of Lloyd-Jones's preaching ministry in the United States is that many of the churches he preached in, had they known his views on the end times, would not have considered him an evangelical. The idea of the Doctor not being evangelical is of course ludicrous. But even today, many churches have the premillennial interpretation of Scripture as part of their denominational basis of faith, and possibly one of the several variants of the tribulation and rapture as well.

In his Great Doctrines series the Doctor went out of his way to be fair to all of the three major interpretations—premillennial, postmillennial, and amillennial. He showed that faithful Christians have believed differently in each of these ways of thinking about the second coming—there is no early church or subsequent evangelical monopoly on any of them. He certainly did *not* say that to believe in one interpretation and not the other two places someone outside of core evangelical belief. In this way he thus differed with many a denomination, especially those that put a particular view into their central doctrines in the twentieth century.

However, it is very plain that he himself fell into the amillennial group. The millennium, in this view, is the time between Christ's ascension and his second coming, and thus all the book of Revelation applies to all believers for all time. For him, this interpretation chimed most with Scripture. And he also felt that there was no detailed description of a rapture in the Bible (except for one way of looking at a particular verse), or in the history of the church, before J. N. Darby and others popularized such a view in the nineteenth century.

People reading this might have strong views in another direction. But we can say that, as in all things, the Doctor based his beliefs on how he interpreted Scripture. However, he enabled his Friday night congregation to understand how the other views also sought biblical justification for their differing interpretation of Scripture. The fact that he did so shows us that this is not an issue upon which evangelicals should divide, let alone break fellowship or deem someone outside the evangelical fold. Thankfully, today many evangelical churches are realizing this. It is the core doctrines of the faith upon which we stand—the existence of judgment and of the second coming—not its timing. Like Capitol Hill Baptist Church, we can be pro-millennial, united rather than divided, on a vexing issue of doctrine.

SUBSTITUTIONARY ATONEMENT AND PROPITIATION

However, on issues such as the substitutionary atonement—which is now disputed among those who have in the past claimed to be evangelical—the Doctor was adamant. There is no room for debate, as the teaching of Scripture upon this matter is abundantly clear. One cannot compromise on why Christ came and what he did for us upon the cross. As he also pointed out, simply because other people refer to the cross in their writings does not make them evangelical; they must show that they believe the teaching of the Bible. As we have seen, the Doctor was quite happy to say that Wesley was evangelical, but those who doubted or played down the doctrine of substitutionary atonement were not.

Recent controversies have shown that some still do not truly understand that Christ came as the *propitiation* for our sins, to propitiate the wrath of God just as the sacrificial animals did in Old Testament times. While the specifics of the current dissent were not around in the Doctor's day—matters that have been dealt with very well by D. A. Carson in recent times—the kind of man-centered heresies alive in the 1950s are not that different from what some now present in different guise. Anyone wanting a guide to what the Bible teaches on propitiation as a doctrine throughout the Bible,

from the dawn of the children of Israel down to Christ's propitia-
tory death on the cross, can do no better than to read the Doctor's
succinct unfolding of the subject.

We could, of course, address many other points of controversy.
But what is important here is to recognize how relevant the Doctor
is for us in the twenty-first century. Even if we disagree with him,
he teaches us to think biblically for ourselves. Fads come and go,
but the truth of God's Word in Scripture is eternal.

10

Conclusion

THE DOCTOR FOR THE
TWENTY-FIRST CENTURY

Though Dr. Martyn Lloyd-Jones died in 1981, he is extraordinarily relevant today. While he spoke to the society in which he lived, it is fascinating to see how what he said then is still true now.

He was a firm believer in preaching. But as the contributors to the anniversary edition of his great apologia, *Preaching and Preachers*, made plain in 2012, the Doctor foresaw many subsequent developments and answered them long before they became infamous. As Kevin DeYoung so rightly points out, his emphasis on preaching as the God-centered way of communicating the truth foreshadows the sad failure of the Emerging Church to understand the power of God in salvation.[1]

The Doctor's stress that the Word of God is *true* was preached before anyone ever heard of postmodernism. But his insistence on that fact—made strongly in his *Truth Unchanged, Unchanging*—reminds us that the postmodernists have got it terribly wrong.

---

[1] D. Martyn Lloyd-Jones, *Preaching and Preachers*, ed. Kevin DeYoung (Grand Rapids, MI: Zondervan, 2011).

The phrase "seeker-sensitive" would have been unfamiliar to him, but the idea that non-Christians in need of repentance and salvation should be made comfortable rather than deeply uncomfortable because of their sin would have been unthinkable to him (as it would have been to fellow London expositor John Stott, who addressed the related "homogenous unit principle").

Fads come and go, but most simply reinvent the wheel. No heresy is actually new. Human beings have been unchanged since the fall. All are fallen sinners in rebellion against God and urgently need reconciliation with him through the complete and finished work of Jesus Christ upon the cross.

Today we find a yearning to come back to the certainties that Dr. Lloyd-Jones stood for and preached for over half a century. Some might dismiss this as a fad, even though they themselves hold strongly to the same Reformed truths the Doctor himself expounded. Since many of the "young, restless, and Reformed" are by definition young and restless, one can see why slightly older folk might be concerned with how long such enthusiasm might last.

However, evangelical leaders such as D. A. Carson, Kevin De-Young, John Piper, Ligon Duncan, Timothy Keller, and Mark Dever are certainly Reformed but neither young nor restless! And it is significant that all but one are contributors to the fortieth anniversary edition of the Doctor's work on preaching. For them he is as much a role model today as ever, and all of them came across his work through reading him in later years; none of them sat under his preaching at Westminster Chapel. Some of the original members of what journalists have called the neo-Calvinists have turned out to be controversial figures, but that description would not apply to any of these men.

John MacArthur, whose views on the Holy Spirit differ from those of the Doctor, is on record as a public admirer of Dr. Lloyd-Jones nonetheless. Even some in the earlier list have written that they would not agree with the Doctor on *all* he said. That is significant. One can still find tremendous values in someone without having to assent to 100 percent of their conclusions—just as many greatly admire John MacArthur without holding to every one of *his* views.

It is significant that sermons that the Doctor preached over half a century are still being read with much enthusiasm by people who were not even born in 1981. New generations are discovering him—even if some think he was a contemporary of Spurgeon's!

It is true that some of what the Doctor thought and spoke about remains relevant only to his time. His controversial views on church separation would fall into that category. It is profoundly encouraging that British evangelicals are now coming back together again not in formal terms, with denominational flags flying, but in *gospel partnerships* based on what they hold in common, rather than on what divides them. Many evangelicals who were always wary of labeling themselves denominationally now make their Bible-based evangelical faith their prime source of identification and fellowship. Similarly, while the issue of the charismatic sign gifts remains as hotly disputed as ever, there are now plenty of groups within that world whose prime self-identification is with fellow evangelicals. This is especially true of groups who hold to a strongly Reformed theology of the doctrines of grace. This is of course deeply sensitive ground! Whether one is a cessationist or a continuationist (like the Doctor), one must ask whether a given experience is biblical or not. Scripture is the measure of all things, and that should always be the benchmark in every situation for all time.

AGREE TO DISAGREE

It is quite possible to agree with Dr. Lloyd-Jones on 90 percent of what he thought and preached while disagreeing with that other 10 percent, provided that the agreement or disagreement is firmly Scripture-based. He has not been served well by those who insist on 100 percent agreement, especially as he never insisted on anything remotely like that himself.

This is an important lesson for how evangelicals handle their heroes. Only God is infallible, and Protestants reject the very notion of the infallibility of the pope. Yet it is often easy to grant quasi-papal status to those who are revered, and in practice we can be no different from those Roman Catholics from whose views Protestants supposedly liberated themselves back at the Reformation. That is why, for instance, the growth of Calvinist Baptists in the United States (in particular those within the Southern Baptist Convention) is so fascinating.

As we have seen, Calvin was a paedobaptist in a way that today's Reformed enthusiasts in the SBC are not. Needless to say, the more strongly Arminian group within the SBC have accused their Reformed brethren of abandoning their Baptist heritage. (Whether that is historically true is an interpretative minefield beyond the purview of this book!) But to the growing number of Reformed pastors and church members within that denomination, what matters is *what the Bible teaches*. And if the doctrines of grace are within the Scriptures and clearly taught there, then that is what they will believe.

In so doing, they are following in the footsteps of Martyn Lloyd-Jones. For Lloyd-Jones, the Bible taught believer's baptism and the doctrines of grace, so that is what evangelical Christians should believe as well. Historically that might be unusual, but evangelical beliefs are Bible-based not man-made.

As always the Doctor was his own man. He preferred sprinkling to full immersion although he agreed with believer's baptism, and while he held that the sign gifts still existed, he never believed that the gift of tongues was a necessary part of the baptism with the Holy Spirit. He was not someone whom one could pigeonhole.

So on two issues, he, the zealous Calvinist and enthusiastic supporter of Reformed theology, rejected two of Calvin's beliefs while agreeing with him fully on the doctrines of grace. Dr. Lloyd-Jones's speech in 1967 on the 450th anniversary of Luther's nailing the ninety-five theses to the Wittenberg door showed how greatly he revered the founder of the Reformation. But on the matter of the

Lord's Supper, for instance, he was firmly opposed to what he considered was Luther's mistaken interpretation. And as a passionate Independent (or Congregationalist), he was equally opposed to Luther's concept of a state church.

As he treated others, so he was happy to be treated himself. He had numerous close friends who were Presbyterians just as he had been in Aberavon. He preached in churches that were cessationist and Pentecostal alike, or who had diverging views from him on eschatological issues. He fully defended Wesley, an Arminian, as a fellow evangelical. He kept Anglican friends though he disagreed with them utterly on their decision to remain within the Church of England.

So now, in a sense, today's evangelicals are catching up with the Doctor. A new generation of Lloyd-Jones enthusiasts have shown how he can be a role model even when they disagree with him on some points. There is no compromise on the gospel itself, on the key evangelical truths embodied in the basis of faith of the International Fellowship of Evangelical Students. Disagreement with that takes someone outside of the evangelical fold. But *within* that framework agreement on the core doctrines can go alongside diversity on other, often deeply held but essentially secondary matters: the mode of baptism, the government of churches, and even the nature of the gifts of the Holy Spirit.

The Doctor considered followers of the Wesley brothers as being within the evangelical family. Not to do so would have been extreme to say the least. The International Fellowship of Evangelical Students had within it those of varying views on the doctrines of grace, and the IFES basis of faith does not comment on them one way or another. In the United States many Methodists still hold passionately to the evangelical faith of their founders; these probably find closer fellowship with evangelicals in Presbyterian or similar groups to than with liberals in their own.

But in helping to revive the interest in Reformed theology after 1945, initially along with J. I. Packer and for decades alongside his close associate and biographer Iain Murray, Dr. Lloyd-Jones surely did the church a favor. How much, one can ask, of what has gone astray in the church worldwide has been because so many evangelicals have been either simply Arminian or Reformed in theory but Arminian in practice?

Also, disciples of his, such as Iain Murray and many in the Free Church part of evangelicalism, clearly show that one can be cessationist *and* have a profound, deep, and what the Puritans would call *experimental* belief in the power of the Holy Spirit. (The same would apply to evangelicals of all stripes in the United States and in the two-thirds world, where British state/free church distinctions do not apply.) Many evangelicals can be so frightened of what they regard as charismatic excess that they go much too far in the opposite direction. Whether one agrees with the Doctor in his interpretation of this controversial issue, one can hopefully go along with him fully in saying that the Scriptures appeal to the mind, the heart, and the will and conscience. A dry and unemotional evangelicalism is surely as wrong as the overemotional and mindless behavior that many rightly deplore.

That is why *logic on fire*, or *theology coming through a man who is on fire*, is the biblical answer, and the one that Martyn Lloyd-Jones sought to emulate all of his ministerial life.

So why have some strayed away to the emerging church? Why attend doctrine-light, seeker-sensitive services? I think much of evangelicalism today lacks the *logic* of Calvin and the *fire* of the Methodist Revival, that unique combination which marked the origins of the Welsh Calvinistic Methodists. This body of believers had tragically lost much of both the logic and the fire by the time that Dr. Lloyd-Jones was a teenager. He would have listened to increasingly political and flowery sermons in London.

Of course many evangelicals remain in that denomination, as his brother-in-law's lifelong attachment to it testifies. But while much of it has left the gospel behind, one could say that the Doctor through his own ministry gave its founding principles a whole new and different lease on life. Some have said that when they *heard* the sermons (now all free to download on MP3), they could sense the fire as well as the logic, which was obvious when they read them in book form.

The Doctor always conveyed a sense of urgency when he preached, and the message he expounded is as urgent today as it ever was. And the gospel is, as he never ceased to proclaim, the *only* answer. It is *God's answer.*

How much of the problems in the church today stem from our having forgotten all this? Take the concept of preaching with *unction.* If God is enabling the preacher to communicate directly to the listeners, with the Holy Spirit already at work in their hearts, wills, and minds, why do we need to be seeker-sensitive? What can be more powerful than the Holy Spirit at work? Why do we need to jettison so much doctrine? Again, it is a failure to understand the power of the Holy Spirit.

Sin is the same as it always was, and the answer in Jesus Christ is the same as well. So why not use God's pattern of "doing church"? For otherwise, we deny the role of God in conversion and the ability of the Holy Spirit to convict and convert. It is not our *felt* needs that matter, but our *objective* need of repentance, since otherwise Christianity is no different from all the postmodern mush so prevalent in our world today.

God knew back when the apostle Paul preached in Athens what the needs of twenty-first-century people in the postmodern West would be. And the model he gave us in Scripture is clearly not intended to change, since people and the human condition do not change. We do not need to modify the Bible in order to get people to hear the gospel and be saved.

None of this is any different from when the Doctor was alive and preaching in Aberavon or in London or around the world. The power of the Holy Spirit is undiminished from the days of the early church. We may not be witnessing revival in Britain or the United States, but many parts of the globe are seeing an amazing outpouring of the work of God, including many places in countries where Christians are being actively persecuted.

We do not need to follow the Doctor in all his practices, but his principles remain as relevant and as Bible-based and Christ-centered as always. While he scorned sermons that he felt were insubstantially short, surely a twenty-five-minute sermon of genuine God-given unction is better than a Lloyd-Jones imitation address of an hour that lacks any of the unction of the original. The Doctor always realized that it was not *his* abilities manifest in the pulpit but a gift and calling from God—not Martyn Lloyd-Jones the *man*, therefore, but Martyn Lloyd-Jones the faithful expositor of the Word of God, called and set apart by God for such a task.

Tim Keller quotes the Doctor as saying that

> the primary object of preaching is not only to give information to be used later, but to make an impression on the heart on the spot. . . . The point of preaching is not just to expound doctrine, but to make the doctrine real to the heart and therefore permanently life-changing.[2]

This is *logic on fire.*

How much is this a reality today, especially for evangelicals who believe that they have the right doctrine? The Doctor's son-in-law Sir Fred Catherwood, who was both a cessationist and a postmillennialist, and involved in politics and social action, differed significantly from his father-in-law in certain areas of biblical interpretation. But Sir Fred, speaking at the Doctor's memorial service in 1981, commented that Dr. Lloyd-Jones was utterly right to say that orthodoxy without life was worthless. One should have both orthodoxy and practice. It was for this that the Doctor strived, especially in the last twenty or so years of his life. One may not agree with all his views, but like Sir Fred, one can passionately agree with the Doctor's principles.

That is why this book has been more discussion than biography,

---

[2] Tim Keller, "A Tract for the Times," in Lloyd-Jones, *Preaching & Preachers*, 94.

although a new generation rediscovering Reformed truths do need to know some of the biographical details before exploring how the Doctor is relevant to our own times. It is also why I have concentrated more on his wider appeal rather than on specifically British-based issues. His Welsh background is fascinating, and it explains much about him, but in terms of how relevant he is to generations around the world born after his death, it is not central to our theme. The same goes for denominational issues, which really applied only in the last fifteen years of his life (1966–1981). These matters are thus less important than his global involvement in evangelical movements such as IFES in which he was deeply engaged for over forty years. It is natural that British authors concentrate on domestic debates, but today the Doctor is well known around the world. His books and now MP3 downloads have made him a truly international figure. And perhaps his being Welsh enabled him to understand non-Anglo-Saxon culture better. Many in IFES certainly felt that this was the case.

So on whatever details people might differ with the Doctor, the key principles upon which he based his life and ministry remain eternal. Mark Dever has written that "Martyn Lloyd-Jones was one of God's special gifts to the church in the twentieth century."[3] And he is still such a gift in the twenty-first. One of the people who knew him best is the Rev. Hywel Jones, who lives in Aberavon in Wales and who also teaches at Westminster Theological Seminary in California. As he put it, Dr. Lloyd-Jones believed in *life*. What a wonderful summary. He believed in the life that God gives us through his Son Jesus Christ, with whom Martyn Lloyd-Jones, his faithful servant, now dwells in eternity.

---

[3] Mark Dever, endorsement of Lloyd-Jones, *Preaching and Preachers*, back cover.

Acknowledgments

One of the most wonderful things about marrying my wife, Paulette, is that my grandmother Bethan Lloyd-Jones lived long enough to see us become engaged and to spend time with her granddaughter-in-law. And as she told my then fiancée, "Martyn would have liked you." That was the ultimate *imprimatur*! Since our marriage in 1991, Paulette has been to me the wonderful and God-given support that Bethan Phillips became to Martyn Lloyd-Jones after the two of them married in 1927. My thanks to Paulette are as profound and devoted as the Doctor's were always to his wife.

My mother, Elizabeth Catherwood, has as always been a tower of support and enthusiasm—in both things she has fully inherited her father's gift of encouragement. I should say of course that the views expressed in this book are my own, and that I speak for myself rather than as a surrogate for any other member of my family.

I am privileged that Crossway is the publisher of this book. They are a godly and thoroughly evangelical publisher who has kept the faith. It is such a joy for the Doctor's family to see so many of his now posthumous works in the hands of a publisher who believes in all the great spiritual truths for which he stood in his lifetime. Warmest thanks go as ever to Lane and Ebeth Dennis, Al Fisher, and Justin Taylor. Tara Davis deserves much gratitude for her detailed editing and Angie Cheatham for her enthusiasm. Thank God for them and all the Crossway team!

I have been most ably supported in prayer by many faithful friends. They have helped many ways that are too numerous to mention, but in order to avoid an overlong acknowledgments section, here are some of them: Nathan and Debbie Buttery; Alasdair and Rachel Paine and their daughters Lucy and Alice; Matthew and Sarah Burling; Richard and Sally Reynolds; Jeremy and Elaine Nunns; Jane Hollis; Juliet Cook; Gill Smith; Matt and Liz Davis; Andrew and Clare Whittaker and their daughters Charlotte and Rosie; Larry and Beth Adams; Claude and Leigh Marshall and their daughters Lauren, Emily (and her husband Eric), and Catherine; Pete Williams; Betsy Weaver Brandt and her husband, Lamar; James and Camilla Ward; and Falcon Green. As for the dedicatees, Don and Emilie Wade: Don is a careful Reformed exegete in the Lloyd-Jones tradition of logic on fire. His wife, Emilie, sat under the Doctor's preaching in the United States and is a personality in the Proverbs 31 mold of Bethan Lloyd-Jones. Both of them have been long-term friends of my wife's and now mine as well. Their theologically informed counsel to us over many decades has been invaluable.

Much of this was written in Churchill College, Cambridge, for which I am most grateful. (I am a Senior Combination Room Associate and Emeritus By-Fellow of the Churchill Archives Centre.) While this particular book was not among those subsidized by the Royal Literary Fund, the fact that I have a grant from them makes writing this book possible.

Bibliography

Atherstone, Andrew, and David Ceri Jones. *Engaging with Martyn Lloyd-Jones: The Life and Legacy of "The Doctor."* Nottingham: Apollos, 2011.

Catherwood, Christopher. *Five Evangelical Leaders.* Wheaton, IL: Harold Shaw, 1985. London: Hodder & Stoughton, 1984.

———. *Martyn Lloyd-Jones: A Family Portrait.* Grand Rapids: Baker, 1995. Eastbourne: Kingsway, 1995.

———. *Martyn Lloyd-Jones: Chosen by God.* Crowborough: Highland Books; Wheaton, IL: Crossway, 1986.

Dever, Mark. "What I've Learned about Preaching from Martyn Lloyd-Jones." In D. Martyn Lloyd-Jones, *Preaching and Preachers*, 40th anniversary edition, edited by Kevin DeYoung, 255–59. Grand Rapids, MI: Zondervan, 2011.

———. Endorsement of D. Martyn Lloyd-Jones, *Preaching and Preachers*, 40th anniversary edition, edited by Kevin DeYoung, 255–59. Grand Rapids, MI: Zondervan, 2011

Evans, Richard. *In Defence of History.* London: Granta Books, 1997.

International Fellowship of Evangelical Students Basis of Faith. http://ifesworld.org/en/our-beliefs.

Jamieson, Bobby. "Biblical Theology and Corporate Worship." *9Marks Journal* (Summer 2014). http://www.9marks.org/journal/biblical-theology-and-corporate-worship.

Keller, Tim. "A Tract for the Times." In D. Martyn Lloyd-Jones, *Preaching and Preachers*, 40th anniversary edition, edited by Kevin DeYoung, 92–94. Grand Rapids, MI: Zondervan, 2011.

Kendall, R. T. *Calvin and English Calvinism to 1649.* London: Paternoster, 1997.

Lloyd-Jones. Bethan. *Memories of Sandfields*. Edinburgh; Carlisle, PA: Banner of Truth, 1983, 2008.

Lloyd-Jones, Martyn. *Acts: Chapters 1–8*. 3 vols. Wheaton, IL: Crossway, 2013. First published in 6 volumes by Banner of Truth (as *Authentic Christianity: Sermons on the Acts of the Apostles* [1999–2006]) and Crossway (as *Studies in the Book of Acts* [2000–2007]).

————. *The Christ-Centered Preaching of Martyn-Lloyd Jones: Classic Sermons for the Church Today*. Edited by Elizabeth Catherwood and Christopher Catherwood. Wheaton, IL: Crossway, 2014.

————. *The Christian Soldier: An Exposition of Ephesians 6:10–20*. Vol. 8 of *Ephesians*. Edinburgh; Carlisle, PA: Banner of Truth, 1977.

————. *The Cross: God's Way of Salvation*, edited by Christopher Catherwood. Wheaton, IL: Crossway, 1986.

————. *Ephesians*. 8 vols. Edinburgh; Carlisle, PA: Banner of Truth, 1972–1982.

————. "Evangelical Unity: An Appeal." In *Knowing the Times: Addresses Delivered on Various Occasions, 1942–1947*, 246–57. Edinburgh; Carlisle, PA: Banner of Truth, 1989.

————. *Evangelistic Sermons from Aberavon*. Edinburgh: Banner of Truth, 1983.

————. *Great Doctrines of the Bible*. 3 vols. London: Hodder and Stoughton, 1996–1998. Also *Great Doctrines of the Bible: Three Volumes in One*. Wheaton: Crossway, 2003.

————. *Life in the Spirit in Marriage, Home and Work: An Exposition of Ephesians 5:18 to 6:9*. Vol. 10 of *Ephesians*. Edinburgh: Banner of Truth; Grand Rapids, MI: Baker, 1973.

————. *Preaching and Preachers*, 40th anniversary edition, edited by Kevin DeYoung. Grand Rapids, MI: Zondervan, 2011.

————. *Revival*. Wheaton, IL: Crossway, 1987.

————. *Romans*. 14 vols. Edinburgh; Carlisle, PA: Banner of Truth, 1970–2003.

————. *The Sons of God: An Exposition of Chapter 8:5–17*. Vol. 10 of *Romans*. Edinburgh; Carlisle, PA: Banner of Truth, 1974.

————. *Spiritual Depression: Its Causes and Cure*. 2nd edition. Grand Rapids, MI: Zondervan, 1998.

———. *Studies in the Sermon on the Mount*. Grand Rapids, MI: Eerdmans, 1959–1960. London: Inter-Varsity, 1959–1960.

———. *Truth Unchanged, Unchanging*. 3rd ed. Bryntirion: Evangelical Press of Wales, 1990. Wheaton, IL: Crossway, 1993. Fearn, Ross-shire: Christian Focus, 2013.

———. "What Is an Evangelical?" In *Knowing the Times: Addresses Delivered on Various Occasions, 1942–1947*. Edinburgh; Carlisle, PA: Banner of Truth, 1989.

———. *Why Does God Allow War? A General Justification of the Ways of God*. Bryntirion: Evangelical Press of Wales, 1986. Wheaton, IL: Crossway, 1994, 2003.

Mather, Cotton. *The Great Works of Christ in America*. 2 vols. Reprint of 1852 ed. Edinburgh: Banner of Truth, 1979.

McGrath, Alister. *To Know and Serve God: A Biography of J. I. Packer*. London: Hodder & Stoughton, 1997.

Murray, Iain H. *David Martyn Lloyd-Jones: The First Forty Years, 1899–1939*. Edinburgh; Carlisle, PA: Banner of Truth, 1982.

———. *David Martyn Lloyd-Jones: The Fight of Faith, 1939–1981*. Edinburgh; Carlisle, PA: Banner of Truth, 1990.

———. *Life of Martyn Lloyd-Jones: 1899–1981*. Edinburgh; Carlisle, PA: Banner of Truth, 2013.

Packer, J. I. *Evangelism and the Sovereignty of God*. Nottingham: Inter-Varsity Press, 2008. Downers Grove, IL: InterVarsity Press, 2012.

Piper, John. "A Passion for Christ-Exalting Power: Martyn Lloyd-Jones on the Need for Revival and Baptism with the Holy Spirit." Paper presented at the Bethlehem Fourth Annual Conference for Pastors, January 30, 1991.

———. "Martyn Lloyd-Jones: The Preacher." In D. Martyn Lloyd-Jones, *Preaching and Preachers*, 40th anniversary edition, edited by Kevin De-Young, 153–55. Grand Rapids, MI: Zondervan, 2011.

Roberts, Vaughan. "Preaching and the Glory of God: The Ministry of Martyn Lloyd-Jones." Talk given at the 2014 Evangelical Ministry Assembly. Proclamation Trust, July 10, 2014. https://www.proctrust.org.uk/resources/. MPEG audio file.

Schaeffer, Francis A. *The Great Evangelical Disaster*. Wheaton, IL: Crossway, 1984.

Index

"When the final chapter of church history is written, I believe Martyn Lloyd-Jones will stand as one of the greatest preachers of all time."

JOHN MACARTHUR

Pastor, Grace Community Church, Sun Valley, California

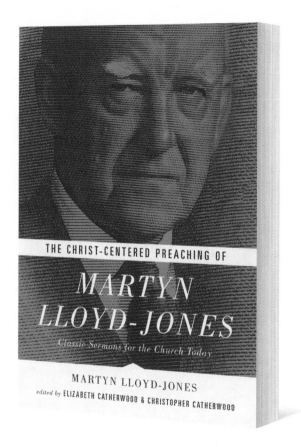

THE CHRIST-CENTERED PREACHING OF

MARTYN LLOYD-JONES

Classic Sermons for the Church Today

MARTYN LLOYD-JONES
edited by ELIZABETH CATHERWOOD & CHRISTOPHER CATHERWOOD

This carefully selected collection of sermons will acquaint you with the life and ministry of famed preacher Dr. Martyn Lloyd-Jones, highlighting each message's historical context and relevance for the church today.